GROWING
tomatoes

your guide to growing delicious tomatoes at home

JASON JOHNS

GroundSwell Books
Summertown, Tennessee

Library of Congress Cataloging-in-Publication Data is available upon request.

We chose to print this title on sustainably harvested paper stock certified by the Forest Stewardship Council, an independent auditor of responsible forestry practices. For more information, visit us.fsc.org.

© 2019 Jason Johns

All rights reserved. No portion of this book may be reproduced by any means whatsoever, except for brief quotations in reviews, without written permission from the publisher.

Cover and interior design: John Wincek
Stock photography: 123 RF

Printed in the United States of America

GroundSwell Books
an imprint of Book Publishing Company
PO Box 99
Summertown, TN 38483
888-260-8458
bookpubco.com

ISBN: 978-1-57067-367-2

24 23 22 21 20 19   1 2 3 4 5 6 7 8 9

CONTENTS

Introduction

Tomatoes are one of the most popular fruits in the world. They are incredibly versatile—delicious both raw and cooked—and they add rich flavor to the foods of many cultures.

Planted in late spring and harvested from midsummer to midautumn, tomatoes are an enjoyable and delicious food to grow in the home garden. Novice gardeners find tomatoes extremely appealing because they're easy to plant, produce good results, and are relatively simple to care for. Besides being a favorite addition to a garden plot, tomatoes can also be grown in pots or hanging baskets, making them an ideal high-yield plant for people without a separate garden.

Commercial tomato farming is done all over the world. In the United States, tomatoes are cultivated extensively in southern states, where a long growing season extends the harvest. However, even vegetable farmers in the colder climates of Michigan and New Jersey grow significant crops of tomatoes at the height of summer.

The tomato is a member of the nightshade (or Solanaceae) family. It's known either by the Latin term that's been popular for the last two centuries, *Lycopersicon esculentum*, or the name many botanists now think is more correct, *Solanum lycopersicum*. Because of how tomatoes are used for culinary purposes, most people refer to them as vegetables, and that's how they're marketed. However, botanists classify tomatoes as fruits because tomatoes are actually the berries of the tomato plant and come from just a single ovary within each tomato flower. (Similarly, peppers and cucumbers are also fruits that masquerade as vegetables.) The tomato was officially classified as a fruit in the US until the late 1800s to avoid taxation, but a Supreme Court ruling deemed the tomato a vegetable so the government could collect much needed taxes from growers.

There's a tomato to suit every need or preference. If size is your concern, you can find a range from small, delicately flavored cherry or baby plum tomatoes to the giant beefsteak tomatoes that are popular either sliced for sandwiches or grilled or stuffed whole and baked. In general, tomatoes are considered to be somewhat sweet, but different varieties have distinctive flavors. Small tomatoes tend to be sweeter than large ones, which can have a slightly acidic or bitter taste. Cooking will temper those acidic flavors, bringing out the tomato's delicious sweetness. Certain varieties of tomatoes make juicy additions to salads, while tomatoes that have a thick flesh, such as Romas, are good candidates for sauces and salsa. Tomatoes also come in a wide range of colors, from red to yellow, orange, and green—and even black, white, purple, and striped! Growing tomatoes of different colors will give you the makings for some interesting dishes, and I always grow several varieties so I can impress houseguests with colored tomato salads.

Tomatoes have to be one of the most eagerly awaited fruits of the summer; being able to pick a ripe tomato and eat it straight from the vine is a wonderful experience that everyone should have. Although you can buy tomatoes from the supermarket throughout the year, the tomatoes you've grown at home or are freshly picked will have the best flavor. If you're buying produce in a market, choose tomatoes that are locally grown and wait until they're in season. Tomatoes grown out of season or transported long distances tend to be more watery and less flavorful. Tomatoes that are sold still on the vine have had more time to ripen naturally and therefore have more flavor than tomatoes that have been picked and transported before they're ripe.

The History of Tomato Cultivation

Tomatoes are strongly associated with Italian cuisine, but they didn't originate in the Mediterranean region. The tomato's ancestral home is thought to have been thousands of miles away in western South America, in areas of Chile, Peru, Ecuador, Columbia, Bolivia, and even the Galapagos Islands!

Though popular in South America, the first cultivated tomatoes are believed to have been small cherry tomatoes grown by the Aztecs in Mexico. The origin of the word tomato is probably from the Aztec *tomatl*, which translates as "the swelling fruit." Tomatoes were not introduced into Europe until seeds were returned to Spain in the sixteenth century by explorers who had visited the New World. The French gave it the name "pomme d'amour," or love apple, because of the tomato's heart shape.

Tomatoes were viewed with suspicion when they were introduced in Europe and were deemed unfit to eat because they're members of the nightshade family. Along with other members of this family—eggplants (aubergine), hot peppers, bell peppers, and potatoes, to name a few—tomatoes were thought to contain suspect, perhaps even dangerous, substances. While tomatoes do contain alkaloids (like one of their more toxic relatives, tobacco), these alkaloids are in such small quantities that virtually everyone can tolerate them.

In sixteenth-century Europe, this exotic new vegetable was primarily afforded by the wealthy. The upper classes often ate off plates made of pewter, which is a lead alloy, and foods that are high in acid (which tomatoes are) leech the lead out of pewter. As a result, consuming tomatoes on pewter plates would cause lead poisoning and, in many cases, death. Wealthy Europeans avoided eating tomatoes until they adopted the use of crockery in the 1800s, yet the poor, who made their plates from wood, enjoyed this culinary delight whenever they could obtain it.

Because the environment around the Mediterranean is very similar to the hot, dry climate of the tomato's home in South America, tomatoes grew easily in this region of Europe. So it's not surprising that they were readily adopted into Italian cuisine. In fact, the growing popularity of tomato consumption in the US in the late 1800s was spurred by the wave of Italian immigrants who brought with them a cuisine rich with tomatoes. Perhaps more importantly, they brought pizza, on which tomato sauce was an essential ingredient. The modern pizza was invented in Naples, as legend has it, to celebrate a visit by Queen Margherita. A restaurant owner was supposed to have created the pizza from three ingredients that were representative of the colors of the new Italian flag. The tomato sauce provided the red, mozzarella cheese the white, and basil leaves scattered on the top represented the green.

Today, according to a 2017 report by the Food and Agriculture Organization, about 170 million tons of tomatoes are grown worldwide. Another report from the University of Florida, also published in 2017, showed that China produced the most tomatoes, followed by the US and India. Other top growing areas included the European Union and Turkey. According to United States Department of Agriculture (USDA) statistics, every single person in the United States ate more than twenty pounds of fresh tomatoes in 2017; when you include processed tomatoes, the figure rises to over ninety pounds per person!

In the US, 80 to 90 percent of the tomato harvest is processed for sauce, juice, or ketchup or is included in ready-to-eat dishes—think frozen pizza. Florida and California are top tomato growing states; in winter, fresh tomatoes are imported from Mexico.

Since the time tomatoes were first cultivated, home growers and horticulturalists have been purposefully selecting particular traits that favor the plant's vigor and enhance the flavor of the fruit. British and New Zealand botanists have recently grafted varieties of tomatoes onto rootstocks of white potatoes, which creates a plant that yields tomatoes above ground and potatoes below—ideal for people who are short on garden space. No matter what type of tomatoes you grow at home, know that the plants you're nurturing have a lineage that goes back thousands of years.

The Health Benefits of Tomatoes

As well as being delicious and versatile, tomatoes are a gold mine of beneficial nutrients. They're packed with antioxidants (such as vitamin C, vitamin E, and beta-carotene) that protect against cell damage, disease, and aging; tomatoes are also good sources of vitamin K and the minerals potassium and manganese. Cuisines that incorporate an abundance of tomatoes, such as those from around the Mediterranean, are linked with increased health and longevity, as well as lower rates of chronic illness.

Tomatoes contain significant amounts of nutrients known to be beneficial for preventing heart disease. One nutrient that's receiving attention from researchers is lycopene, a powerful antioxidant. Lycopene decreases the damage done to cell walls by oxygen; if left unchecked, this damage can cause atherosclerosis, the dangerous buildup of plaque in arteries. Lycopene is also good for bone health. In a Chinese study done in 2013, it was shown that after four weeks, women who didn't have lycopene in their diet had increased levels of oxidative stress and weaker bones compared to women who had been taking lycopene.

Another way tomatoes contribute to heart health is by regulating fats in the bloodstream—specifically, reducing both bad cholesterol (LDL) levels and triglycerides. Researchers are currently investigating two phytonutrients found in tomatoes: a saponin called esculeoside A that's been shown to reduce arterial damage from plaques, and another substance called 9-oxo-octadecadienoic acid that helps encourage chemical interactions in cells. Tomatoes also contain anti-aggregatory phytonutrients that help prevent platelets in the blood from clumping together and causing unwanted clotting.

Although scientists are testing the use of isolated lycopene to prevent heart disease, this compound might be more effective when acting synergistically with the other beneficial nutrients found in tomatoes. Heating lycopene appears to concentrate it and makes it easier for the body to absorb. In order to get more of the benefits of lycopene, be sure to consume tomato sauce, ketchup, tomato juice, and tomato soup on a regular basis!

Tomatoes are also shown to protect against cancer because they reduce oxidative stress and inflammation in cells. It's been shown that a nutrient in tomatoes called alpha-tomatine can significantly lower the risk of prostate cancer in men. This substance can change the metabolic activity of prostate cancer cells as they develop and can trigger programmed cell death in fully formed cancer cells.

Alpha-tomatine also appears to be effective against lung, breast, and pancreatic cancers.

A wide range of studies done in the last decade in the US, Europe, and Japan show that tomatoes have a positive effect on weight control. For instance, the fiber in tomatoes makes people feel more full, the lycopene they contain helps metabolize fats, and overall, the nutrients in tomatoes can increase metabolism. There's growing evidence that obesity is linked to inflammation and oxidative stress, and a recent Brazilian study demonstrates how well lycopene fights that stress. Korean researchers are even looking at the nutrients in tomatoes as possible candidates in the fight against Alzheimer's disease.

The information that follows will help you successfully grow your own delicious tomatoes at home. You'll learn everything you need to know, from selecting the best variety for your specific needs to the best way to get your plants in the ground, protect them from pests and disease, harvest them—and even what to do with your bumper crop as it overflows your counters! Whether you're growing tomatoes yourself or with children, I know you'll enjoy the process and love what you can do with the abundance of fruits your tomato plants produce.

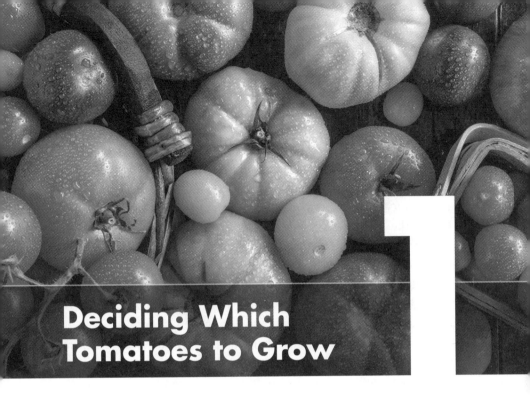

Deciding Which Tomatoes to Grow

A look through any vegetable seed catalog will convince you that the number of different types of tomatoes available is astounding. How do you decide which varieties are the best choices for you? If you're a novice gardener, start with types that grow well in your area. How hot are your summers, do you receive much rainfall, and how long is your growing season? You'll want to make sure your plants will thrive in your climate and will mature before cold weather sets in. Do you live so far north that you might need plants that mature quickly or have to grow your plants in a small greenhouse?

Then think about how you plan to use your tomatoes. Are you growing tomatoes to use fresh in salads, do you want to make your own tomato sauce or juice, or are there young children who would love small tomatoes as finger food? Some tomatoes are juicy, while others are pulpy. Some plants will grow tomatoes so large you can cut slices big enough to cover a burger. Then there are varieties that will yield dozens and dozens of bite-size tomatoes as sweet as candy.

Once you've made practical choices, don't forget to have some fun. You'll find both seeds and plants for tomatoes that grow in a range of colors not usually seen in supermarket, such as orange, purple, or striped.

Deciding Between Hybrids and Heirlooms

All tomato varieties began as wild plants whose properties were shaped over thousands of years by human selection and cultivation. Ancient gardeners saved seeds from fruits whose characteristics (or the characteristics of the parent plant) they preferred. The plants that resulted eventually came to be known as heirloom varieties. Modern botanists discovered how to cross-pollinate different varieties by hand to create plants that would develop particular traits, although the traits would not reliably pass down through the seeds of those plants. These were known as hybrid varieties.

Tomato seeds come either from modern hybrid plants that produce uniformly shaped tomatoes or heirloom plants, which produce fruits that are more unusual, have interesting flavors, and come in all sorts of sizes, shapes, and colors.

Hybrid seeds are usually referred to as F1 seeds, which stands for filial 1 or "first children." They come from plants that have been cross-pollinated by hand to ensure the resulting seeds take on the best qualities of each plant. The principle advantage of F1 seeds is they often produce plants that are disease and pest resistant. If you live where tomato blight is prevalent, buying an F1 variety bred for blight resistance may mean you can grow tomatoes to maturity. (See pages 76 and 77 for more information on blight.) Other advantages are that the fruit from hybrid seeds are very uniform in appearance and flavor and the plants generally produce higher, more consistent yields. Commercial growers are particularly interested in uniformity and consistency, as this maximizes the amount of money they can make from their crops.

The downsides of F1 seeds are that the adult plants that grow from these seeds are frequently sterile and the seeds of hybrid fruits don't produce the original strain of the parent hybrid plant. Many gardeners don't like to grow F1 strains because they have to buy seeds year after year. To plant a desired hybrid variety, growers have to purchase more of that variety seed, which is a great benefit for the seed company but not the grower who prefers to save seeds from year to year. F1 seeds tend to be more expensive than heirloom varieties because they're produced scientifically. Although many F1 varieties will mature faster than their heirloom cousins, many growers feel that the flavor of F1 varieties is not as robust.

Many tomato experts will tell you that hybrid tomatoes are bland—lacking the flavor they'd have from the sugars that develop while they're left on the vine—because they're bred to be picked while green and ripened during shipping. Hybrids are typically bred for commercial growers to create high yields of fruits that ripen at more or less the same time, which is what a commercial grower needs. If you're growing tomatoes for canning, this might be beneficial for you, but if you want a steady supply of eating tomatoes, you'll be left with a sudden glut you won't be able to keep up with.

Hybrid plants certainly have their advantages and, in the right environment, are worth growing. However, in this book we're going to focus on heirloom varieties. Heirloom tomatoes have been grown for decades, if not hundreds of years. They're especially tasty and are best eaten right out of the garden—or at least within a few days. Many gardeners like the natural differences and rich flavor found in heirloom fruit, qualities that are especially appreciated by experienced growers. For me, the advantages of heirloom tomatoes are that they come in interesting colors and sizes, and the varieties have a long and interesting history. Most people don't think tomatoes come in any color other than red, so when I serve yellow, orange, black, or striped tomatoes, people are always impressed and want to know more about them. If you start cultivating unusual heirlooms, other gardeners will want to strike up a conversation with you once they see what you're growing.

Heirloom tomatoes are becoming increasingly popular as more and more people want to get back to basics and move away from standardization. Because heirlooms don't normally travel or store particularly well, you may never see these varieties in a local supermarket unless it has a specialty produce section—and then they'll be quite expensive. Sometimes you can find them in local farmers' markets. The tomatoes on an heirloom plant tend to ripen at different times, which gives you a longer picking season and puts less pressure on you to store and preserve everything at once.

The seeds for heirlooms are usually cheaper than those for hybrids because the plants are open-pollinated—pollinated naturally by bees rather than cross-pollinated by hand. Open-pollination can provide opportunities for interesting new varieties to develop and allows you to save the seeds for growing your own plants the following year (see page 83). You can then breed your own varieties of tomatoes or grow more of the tomatoes you enjoy without having to spend more money on seeds.

Different varieties of heirloom plants thrive in different conditions; some like sun, some like cool climates, and some are more disease resistant than others. If you buy seeds that are grown in your area, there's a good chance they'll be more resistant to local pests and problems. Heirloom tomatoes also tend to have all the healthful nutritional qualities associated with tomatoes (see pages 4 to 6) because they haven't had those qualities bred out of them in the search for fruit that will be uniform and stand up to commercial conditions.

My personal preference is for heirloom tomatoes, and I would recommend them to anyone. The variety, flavor, and enjoyment you'll get from these fruits will make growing them well worth your while. For me, there's something quite pleasurable about growing purple tomatoes or yellow tomatoes. Once your friends try your homegrown tomatoes, they'll be hooked, and I can guarantee they'll either be visiting you more during tomato season or wanting tips on how grow their own!

Grafted tomatoes

You might also find grafted tomato plants in specialty garden shops. With a grafted tomato, one type of fruiting tomato is grafted onto the rootstock of a different type. This allows a plant that would normally be a rambling vine to be grown on a bushy rootstock or for a slow-fruiting variety to be grown on a rapidly growing rootstock. (The roots will determine the size of the plant, and the graft will determine the types of fruit.) The most common grafted plants are tomato varieties with unusual colors, often black tomatoes.

Selecting a Type

Although there are many different varieties of tomatoes, there are just four different types, which relate to the size of the fruit and the growing pattern of the plants. All of the different varieties fall into one of these five types.

CLASSIC (SALAD) TOMATOES

These are the tomatoes you're most familiar with and see most often in supermarkets. They're the classic red, round tomatoes that can be used fresh in salads and for baking, frying, grilling, and other cooked dishes. Classic tomatoes are the most common varieties grown at home, and there's a huge range from which to choose.

CHERRY AND COCKTAIL TOMATOES

Cherry tomatoes are smaller versions of classic tomatoes and are common in supermarkets. Cocktail tomatoes are slightly larger than cherry tomatoes, though the two are sometimes sold under the same name. They come in a number of dif-

ferent colors, including red, orange, yellow, and golden, and heirloom varieties are available. Sometimes cherry tomatoes are sold while still on the vine, although most commonly they're sold in baskets or containers.

Cherry tomatoes are very sweet, with a concentrated flavor. They're great eaten whole and raw and are ideal for salads and lunch boxes. Their size and flavor make them a favorite with children. You can grill cherry tomatoes whole or halved, cook with them, or make sauces from them.

PLUM, BABY PLUM, PEAR, AND GRAPE TOMATOES

Plum tomatoes are undoubtedly one of the most popular types for cooking because they contain more flesh and less water than classic

tomatoes. If you enjoy making your own tomato sauce and ketchup, you'll enjoy growing some of these.

Plum tomatoes are oval and very firm, making them ideal for grilling. They're also popular for making pizza sauces or for use in pasta dishes. Because of their growing popularity, more supermarkets are carrying them in season. Pear tomatoes are a variation on the plum tomato and are more pear shaped rather than oval. Both pear and plum tomatoes are commonly

used in Italian cuisine because of their thick flesh.

Baby plum tomatoes are a hit with children because they're sweet, firm, not too juicy, and easy for small fingers to manage. You'll often see small plum tomatoes referred to as grape tomatoes because of their shape.

BEEFSTEAK TOMATOES

Beefsteak (or beef) tomatoes are much larger than salad tomatoes, sometimes massively so. They can grow to a huge size, weighing

in at several pounds each. They're ideal for baking whole or stuffed, and there are a variety of different kinds on the market, including some that are pink and even one that's yellow, called Yellow Beefsteak, with a hybrid version called Colossal.

Beefsteak tomatoes can be found at supermarkets and farmers' markets but are less common than classic or cherry tomatoes. They used to be only available in season, but now that they're grown and shipped all over the world, you can find them year round. They're usually sold as single tomatoes.

Vine or truss tomatoes

These are any of the previous types sold while still attached to the fruiting stem. They're marketed as fresher and better for you because they haven't been detached from the vine. Vine tomatoes have a richer aroma (because of the attached stem) and strong tomato taste, making them the choice of many people for salads and cooking. They're more expensive than salad tomatoes because it's more difficult to transport them without spoilage.

Vine tomatoes can be confused with vine-ripened tomatoes, which are those that are left to ripen on the plant and picked when they're ripe. While this practice does make tomatoes tastier, they become more perishable and can't be shipped long distances. In the UK, all tomatoes are vine-ripened as they don't have a long way to travel, though imported tomatoes and some tomatoes sold in the US are picked before they're ripe so they can survive the journey to stores without spoiling.

Vine tomatoes need to be left on the vine until you're ready to use them; they'll deteriorate quite quickly when they're removed from the stalk. You can keep the end of the stalk in water, which will keep the fruit moist while it's stored, but it won't last this way for long and the stem can sometimes develop mold.

Many gardeners will grow a few tomato plants from all these types, depending on their individual preferences. At the very least, try some cherry tomatoes and classic tomatoes; as you gain experience, you may be tempted by plums and beefsteaks. Certainly, grow what you eat and enjoy, but consider being adventurous and try something new for variety. Every year I grow a variety that's new to me, especially one I can't buy at my local supermarket. Heirloom tomatoes are my favorites because of their taste and variety of shapes and colors, although occasionally I'll grow F1 varieties if I'm looking for a yield that will ripen all at once for canning.

Not All Tomatoes Are Red

Many people are surprised to discover that tomatoes come in a rainbow of colors and not just red. A browse through any seed catalog will show that tomatoes come in an incredible range of colors. Different varieties within each color group have different flavors and other characteristics. In the table on pages 21 to 26, you'll find tomatoes of every color listed among the most popular varieties grown in the US. In the section that follows, I'll also tell you about some varieties that might be less familiar or are grown in other areas of world but that merit attention.

PINK OR RED TOMATOES

These are the types of tomatoes you're used to seeing on grocery shelves. They're also the most common varieties found in garden supply centers. While you can readily buy these in any supermarket, the taste of a freshly picked, homegrown tomato is so much better and one of the greatest pleasures a gardener can experience.

One of the classic favorites is Brandywine. The plants grow huge vines up to ten feet tall that will bend almost to the ground under the weight of the fruit. Red Brandywine produces slightly smaller fruits but is much more disease resistant than the standard Brandywine.

Two varieties that are equally delicious but ripen slightly earlier are German Johnson and Pruden's Purple, though the latter is more susceptible to disease. Anna Russian is a popular oxheart type (slightly pointed at the bottom) that is well worth trying due to its flavor.

Eva Purple Ball produces fruits the size of a baseball is very disease tolerant and also quite adaptable to different weather, meaning it's a great plant to grow in northern areas. Other varieties that are particularly suited for cool northern areas are Marianna's Peace, Crnkovic Yugoslavian, and Aunt Ginny's Purple.

By planting early varieties as well as later varieties, you'll get a steady crop of tomatoes throughout the growing season. German Red Strawberry, Vintage Wine (pink with gold streaks), and Marizol Purple are great early croppers that are full of flavor.

Hybrid tomatoes such as Big Beef, Celebrity, Better Boy, and Mountain Fresh are widely available and produce large, uniformly shaped fruits. Better Boy is of particular interest for its disease resistance and the fact that it will keep on cropping until hit by frost.

BLACK, PURPLE, OR BROWN TOMATOES

These dark tomatoes have become more popular in recent years because of their color. They're very tasty and look great in a salad, inspiring interest and comments whenever they're served. Typically, the darker the tomatoes are, the more acidic the flavor.

Cherokee Purple is a very popular tomato with a well-balanced flavor that is sweet and almost wine-like. It's naturally disease tolerant and produces an abundance of fruit quite early in the season. It has deep purple skin, green marbled flesh, and looks great in a salad when mixed with other colored tomatoes. Another popular early and tasty tomato is Black Sea Man.

Black Prince is a heavy cropper of greenish-brown tomatoes that are full of juice and around the size of a tennis ball! These are delicious tomatoes with a wonderful taste, but they do tend to crack in rainy weather.

Lesser known varieties that are very tasty and heavy croppers include Ananas Noire and Sara Black, both of which are worth looking for. The seeds are not common in garden supply stores but are easily found online.

WHITE TOMATOES

White tomatoes tend to be very sweet, though still acidic. Combine these with other colored tomatoes, and you can have a very full-flavored rainbow salad.

White Wonder has a mild flavor that will balance the heartier taste of larger tomatoes, though some people say it's a bit bland. White Queen is another popular variety with bolder flavor than White Wonder.

White tomatoes tend to be quite rare, as there aren't many varieties available. Your best bet is to look for seeds online.

YELLOW OR ORANGE TOMATOES

There's a plethora of yellow, orange, and even striped tomatoes on the market. You'll have to grow most of these from seed, though occasionally you can find yellow tomato seedlings in specialty garden centers.

Hugh's is an incredibly popular variety, as it produces lots of giant yellow tomatoes that are juicy and very tasty. They're so sweet you can almost eat them like apples! Yellow Brandywine is a much firmer fruit with a sweet flavor and good yields. It's late to ripen and doesn't appreciate being outside until the weather is warm. Yellow Brandywine is also a very good variety for growing in a greenhouse and will thrive in the warmer conditions of an extended growing season.

Orange Strawberry is a rich, meaty tomato that does well in northern regions, as it requires a shorter growing season than other tomatoes. Lillian's Yellow Heirloom is another tasty tomato that has a high yield and good disease tolerance.

If you like cherry tomatoes, then Taxi is a great early cropper that starts to die back when main season varieties are ripening. A larger and later variety is Mountain Gold, which also is resistant to diseases.

For beefsteak tomato lovers, Azoychka is a delicious yellow heirloom variety that ripens relatively early in the season. Verna Orange is another good variety, producing large meaty fruits in great quantity that are perfect for both eating fresh and cooking.

GREEN TOMATOES

Green tomatoes are another unusual type that will provoke interest and conversation at your dinner table, especially in a mixed tomato salad. A true green tomato is not merely an unripe tomato, and beginners can find it confusing to know when these varieties are ripe. Depending on the variety of green tomato (virtually all of which have been bred by humans), they can take on a hint of color from an ancestor plant as they ripen, perhaps becoming slightly red or yellow. It can be difficult to know when they're ripe, but unripe tomatoes are firm, ripe ones have a little give to them, and overripe tomatoes are very squishy. You might have to get used to the idea of eating a fresh tomato that's green, because we're so conditioned to only eat green tomatoes if they've been cooked.

Green Zebra

Green Zebra

A rich, sweet-tasting variety is Green Zebra, which has a rather nice salty tang. It's susceptible to blossom end rot, so it needs careful watering. The Green Zebra prefers slightly cooler climates, being fine somewhere like Wisconsin, and will struggle in southern states.

Aunt Ruby's German Green doesn't blush yellow like many other green tomatoes, so you have to check if it's ripe by giving it a slight squeeze. Green Giant is a delicious tomato; although it's a relative newcomer to the market, it's proving to be a big winner. It's a vigorous and prolific fruiter, very popular with gardeners.

BI-COLOR TOMATOES

There are some very intriguing varieties that come in a range of color combinations. You'll find yellow tomatoes with veins of red that are striking and tasty and make intriguing additions to tomato salads. Some bi-color tomatoes are orange with dark red stripes, and there are other color varieties (such as black and orange and green and orange), giving you a nice mix of different colored tomatoes.

Some of the most popular varieties include the Georgia Streak, Pineapple, Striped German, and Peppermint, all of which are good growers and tasty. Peppermint is particularly well suited for cool climates.

There are many different types of tomatoes on the market, and you can have great fun picking the seeds you want to grow. Many

of the more interesting varieties will not be available as seedlings, so you'll need to order them online and germinate them yourself

You can use one of the many specialty plant growers or even find plenty of interesting, good-quality seeds (see the references on page 113). Whichever type you decide on, check the instructions on the seed packets, as some of the more unusual varieties may have specific soil or germination requirements you'll need to follow.

Popular Tomato Varieties in the US

There are a lot of different tomato cultivars, plants that have been grown for their particular characteristics, and you'll have hours of fun selecting the ones you want to grow. Note that tomato plants grow in two forms: determinate and indeterminate. Determinates are compact bush tomatoes, while indeterminates are the vining varieties you need to pinch back in order to remove side shoots (see page 44).

Although you can try to grow almost any tomato in any area, you'll have more success and get a better yield if you choose a variety that's best suited for your particular area. For instance, growing a variety that likes plenty of heat will not work in a cool environment unless you're growing it in a greenhouse. In the pages that follow, you'll learn about varieties that are suited for different climates in the US, as well as varieties that are bred to resist common tomato diseases or will flourish in baskets or containers.

BEST TOMATOES TO GROW IN THE SOUTH

Tomatoes grown in southern states must be able to withstand hot temperatures. When tomato plants are exposed to temperatures that are too warm for them, they'll often drop their flowers or have problems setting fruit. The best tomatoes for the South are heat and drought tolerant.

Southerners will often bemoan that "it's not the heat, it's the humidity," and so it is for tomatoes. High levels of humidity create ideal conditions for the disease known as blight that's so very difficult to control and often shortens the growing season. Both early and late blight are common, more so in warm, wet summers. The table on pages 21 to 26 will list those varieties that are blight resistant and should be grown in areas where blight is prevalent. (See pages 76 and 77 for more information on blight.)

BEST TOMATOES FOR HOT, DRY CLIMATES

Hot, dry climates challenge gardeners not only with drought and high temperatures but often with high winds and poor quality soils as well. Fortunately, there are plants that will thrive (or at least survive) under these conditions. Tomatoes that flower quickly will do well in a desert environment because they produce fruit that's ready to pick before temperatures become extreme and blight sets in. Tomato plants with particularly thick stems are better at withstanding the wind and exposure that's common in these hot, dry environments.

BEST TOMATOES FOR COLDER CLIMATES

If you live in a cool environment, you might think you have to grow tomatoes in a greenhouse in order to be successful. While this will help you grow some of the more exotic tomatoes, new varieties have been developed that grow well in cool areas. If you're growing tomatoes outside, opt for types that set fruit in cool temperatures and mature quickly, before winter frost hits.

BLIGHT-RESISTANT TOMATO VARIETIES

Blight is a very common problem that can strike anytime. (For more information, see pages 76 and 77.) Unfortunately, once you have blight, you're unlikely to ever get rid of it. There are two types of blight, early and late, caused by different types of fungi. Early blight affects the stems and leaves, so plants don't produce as much fruit as they should. Late blight can destroy a plant in just a few days, and you end up with spots or mold on the fruit and leaves. While blight-resistant tomato varieties are not immune to early blight or late blight, they have more resilience than other types of tomatoes, so you'll have a better chance of cultivating a healthy crop.

Developing blight-resistant tomatoes is big business for agronomists, especially as more and more areas are affected by blight. Because blight can decimate a crop, resistant varieties can make or break a commercial tomato-growing operation. Similarly for the home gardener, growing a variety with some resistance can make the difference between harvesting some tomatoes and disposing of diseased plants.

BEST TOMATOES FOR CONTAINERS

Not everyone has the space or optimal soil and sunlight for growing tomatoes directly in the ground. If you find yourself shy of good garden space, container gardening could be a viable solution. Most tomato varieties will work if you have a large enough pot. Some varieties will grow well in containers that hold at least five gallons, whereas others prefer larger containers for spreading their roots. The biggest challenge with container growing is that your plant will have limited access to nutrients and water, so it will be necessary to water it frequently and feed it regularly.

BEST TOMATOES FOR HANGING BASKETS

Bush and tumbling tomatoes (a type that grows many short stems rather than long vines) do very well in hanging baskets, which are ideal for people without the space for large containers. You don't need to stake tomatoes in hanging baskets, as the foliage will just tumble over the edges and hang down. Shallow-rooted varieties do best in this type of container.

BEST VARIETIES TO GROW IN THE US

VARIETY	DESCRIPTION	DAYS TO MATURITY	DISEASE RESISTANCE*
POPULAR HYBRIDS			
Better Boy	Indeterminate, red, beefsteak	75	V, F, N
Big Beef	Indeterminate, red, beefsteak	73	V, FF, N, T, A
Big Boy	Indeterminate, red, beefsteak	78	A
Celebrity	Determinate, red, globe	70	V, FF, N, TA
Early Girl	Indeterminate, smaller, red, globe	50 to 52	V, FF
Grape	Indeterminate, red, cherry	60	F, A
Independence Day	Indeterminate, small, red, globe	49	None
Jersey	Determinate, small, red, globe	75	V, F, A
Juliet	Indeterminate, very small, red, cherry	60	Crack resistant, early blight resistant, late blight resistant
Sun Sugar	Indeterminate, orange, cherry	62	F, T
POPULAR OPEN-POLLINATED OR HEIRLOOM			
Amish Paste	Indeterminate, red, paste	85	Susceptible to cracking and sunscald due to sparse foliage
Black Krim	Indeterminate, red to brown, beefsteak	69 to 80	F, N
Brandywine	Indeterminate, pink, beefsteak	69 to 80	F
Cherokee Purple	Indeterminate, black-purple, beefsteak	69 to 80	F
Green Zebra	Determinate, small, green	78	None
Mortgage Lifter	Indeterminate, large, pink, beefsteak	85	V, F, N
San Marzano	Indeterminate, small, pink-red, plum	85	Traditionally no resistance, modern hybrids have VF resistance bred into them
Yellow Pear	Indeterminate, small, pear-shaped, yellow, cherry	71	V, FF

V - Verticillium wilt	A - Alternaria alternata (stem canker or early blight)	*(See more about plant diseases on pages 74 to 81.)*
F - Fusarium wilt		
FF - Fusarium wilt races 1 and 2	T - Tobacco mosaic virus	
N - Nematodes	St - Stemphylium (gray leaf spot)	

VARIETY	DESCRIPTION	DAYS TO MATURITY	DISEASE RESISTANCE*
POPULAR IN SOUTHERN STATES			
Better Boy	Indeterminate, red, globe	75	V, F, N, A
Mountain Supreme	Determinate, red, globe	69 to 80	V, F, blight
Solar Set	Determinate, medium, red, globe	70	V, FF
Sunmaster	Determinate, medium, red, globe	72	V, FF, A, St
Sweet Million	Indeterminate, red, cherry	75	V, FF, N, T, St, crack resistant
BEST HEIRLOOMS FOR SOUTHERN STATES			
Arkansas Traveler	Indeterminate, medium, pink	75 to 90	Crack resistant
No disease resistance specified, but growers report it has good general resistance			
Brandywine	Indeterminate large, pink, beefsteak	69 to 80	F
Dad's Mug	Indeterminate, conical, pink-red, oxheart	85	None
San Marzano	Indeterminate, small, pink-red, plum	85	Traditionally no resistance, modern hybrids have VF resistance bred into them
BEST FOR HOT, DRY CLIMATES			
Beefmaster	Indeterminate, very large, deep red, beefsteak	80	V, F, N, A, St
Celebrity	Determinate, red, globe	70	V, FF, N, T, A
Early Girl	Indeterminate, smaller, red, globe	50 to 52	V, FF
Sweet 100	Indeterminate, red, cherry	65	V, F
BEST HEIRLOOMS FOR HOT, DRY CLIMATES			
Arkansas Traveler	Indeterminate, medium, pink	90	Crack resistant
No disease resistance specified, but growers report it has good general resistance			
Brandywine off the Vine	Indeterminate, large, red, beefsteak	72	None
Burbank Slicing	Determinate, red, globe	70	Crack resistant
Costoluto Genovese	Indeterminate, large, red	85	Resistant to botrytis and bacterial leaf spot
Eva Purple Ball	Indeterminate, small, red-purple, globe	78	Late blight
GENERALLY DISEASE RESISTANT			
Great White Beefsteak	Indeterminate, large, white, beefsteak	80	Sunscald, crack resistant

VARIETY	DESCRIPTION	DAYS TO MATURITY	DISEASE RESISTANCE*
DROUGHT RESISTANT			
Marvel Striped	Indeterminate, large, bi-color, beefsteak	95	None
Purple Calabash	Indeterminate, medium, fluted oblate, purple or burgundy, beefsteak	85 to 90	Drought tolerant
CRACK RESISTANT			
Thessaloniki	Indeterminate, red, globe	80	Sunscald, crack resistant
BEST OPEN-POLLINATED (OP) FOR HOT, DRY CLIMATES			
Homestead 24	Determinate, medium, red, globe	80	F, A
Porter/Porter Improved	Indeterminate, medium, pink-red, plum	72 to 78	V, F
Prize of the Trials	Indeterminate, large, orange, cherry	80	Crack resistant
Roma VF	Determinate, red, plum	75	V, F
BEST FOR COLD CLIMATES			
Celebrity	Determinate, large, red, globe	70	V, FF, N, T, A
Golden Nugget	Determinate, small, yellow, cherry	60	V
Husky Gold	Indeterminate, medium, gold, globe	69-80	V, F, A
Orange Pixie	Determinate, large yellow-orange, cherry	52	V, F, T
Oregon Spring	Determinate, red, globe	58 to 60	V
Siletz	Determinate, large, red, globe	52 to 75	V, F
BEST HEIRLOOMS FOR COOL CLIMATES			
Bush Beefsteak	Determinate, deep red, beefsteak	62 to 72	None
Galina	Indeterminate, small, yellow/ orange, cherry	69 to 80	Crack resistant
Glacier	Determinate, small, red, globe	55	Cold tolerant, has been known to survive light frosts
Gregori's Altai	Indeterminate, oblate, pink-red, beefsteak	69 to 80	Drought tolerant

V - Verticillium wilt
F - Fusarium wilt
FF - Fusarium wilt races 1 and 2
N - Nematodes

A - Alternaria alternata
    (stem canker or early blight)
T - Tobacco mosaic virus
St - Stemphylium (gray leaf spot)

(See more about plant diseases on pages 74 to 81.)

VARIETY	DESCRIPTION	DAYS TO MATURITY	DISEASE RESISTANCE*
HEAT TOLERANT			
Grushovka	Determinate, egg-shaped, pink	65	None
Kimberly	Indeterminate, small, red, cherry	55 to 68	None
Legend	Determinate, very large, red, beefsteak	68	Blight
Manitoba	Determinate, red, globe	58	V, F
New Yorker	Determinate, scarlet, beefsteak	66	V, A
Polar Baby	Determinate, small, red, globe	55 to 68	None
Polar Beauty	Determinate, small, red, globe	63	Drought tolerant
Polar Star	Determinate, small, red, globe	65	None
Sasha's Altai	Indeterminate, medium, red, globe	60	None
Siberian	Determinate, small, egg-shaped, bright red	50	None
Silvery Fir Tree	Determinate, medium, orange-red	55 to 60	Good general disease resistant
Stupice	Indeterminate, medium, red	55 to 65	None
Sugar Baby	Determinate, large, orange, cherry	54	None
BEST HYBRIDS FOR CONTAINERS			
Big Boy Bush	Determinate, large, red, globe	72	V, F, N, T
Bush Goliath	Determinate, red, globe	68	V, F, N
Celebrity	Determinate, large, red, globe	70 to 72	V, F, N, T
Early Girl Bush	Semi-determinate, small, red, cherry	65	V, F, A
Patio F	Determinate, red, globe	70	F
Sweet 100	Indeterminate, tiny, red, cherry	65	V, F, N, T
Sweet Baby Girl	Indeterminate, dark red, cherry	65	F, T
Window Box Roma	Determinate, red, plum	70	V, F, N
BEST HEIRLOOMS FOR CONTAINERS			
Green Zebra	Determinate, small, green	78	None
Japanese Black Trifele	Indeterminate, pear-shaped, magenta-black	85	Crack resistant
Manitoba	Determinate, medium, crimson	58	V, F
Principe Borghese	Determinate, small, red, plum	69 to 80	Hardy and heat tolerant
Sprite	Determinate, red, grape	60	None

VARIETY	DESCRIPTION	DAYS TO MATURITY	DISEASE RESISTANCE*
RESISTANT TO EARLY BLIGHT			
Juliet	Indeterminate, hybrid, small, elongated, red, cherry	60	Cracking
Legend	Determinate, open-pollinated, large, red, beefsteak	68	Also late blight
Manalucie	Indeterminate, hybrid, red, globe	82	Gray leaf mold, fusarium wilt, and blossom end rot
Manyel	Indeterminate, heirloom, large, golden yellow, globe	75	None
Matt's Wild Cherry	Indeterminate, heirloom, small, red	70	Good general disease resistance
Mountain Fresh Plus	Determinate, hybrid, large, red, globe	77	V, FF, N, blossom end rot
Mountain Supreme	Determinate, hybrid, red, globe	70	V, F
Old Brooks	Indeterminate, heirloom, medium, red, globe	78	Late blight and blossom end rot resistant
RESISTANT TO LATE BLIGHT			
Fantasio	Indeterminate, hybrid, medium, red, globe	80 to 90	V, F, N, T
Ferline	Indeterminate, hybrid, deep-red, globe	95	V, F
Golden Sweet	Indeterminate, hybrid, deep yellow, grape	60	Cracking
Legend	Determinate, open-pollinated, large, red, beefsteak	68	Also early blight
Old Brooks	Indeterminate, heirloom, medium, red, globe	78	Also early blight and blossom end rot
BEST HYBRIDS FOR HANGING BASKETS			
Floragold Basket	Determinate, yellow-orange ,cherry	55	None
Florida Basket	Determinate, red, plum	70	Gray leaf spot
Micro-Tom	Determinate, small, red, cherry	85 to 88	F, St
Red Robin	Determinate, dwarf, red, cherry	55	Crack resistant
Tumbling Tom	Determinate, red and yellow, cherry	70	V, F, N

V - Verticillium wilt
F - Fusarium wilt
FF - Fusarium wilt races 1 and 2
N - Nematodes

A - Alternaria alternata
    (stem canker or early blight)
T - Tobacco mosaic virus
St - Stemphylium (gray leaf spot)

(See more about plant diseases on pages 74 to 81.)

VARIETY	DESCRIPTION	DAYS TO MATURITY	DISEASE RESISTANCE*
BEST HEIRLOOMS FOR HANGING BASKETS			
Baxter's Early Bush Cherry	Determinate, red, cherry	72	Split resistant
Whippersnapper	Determinate, small, pink-red, cherry	52	None

V - Verticillium wilt

F - Fusarium wilt

FF - Fusarium wilt races 1 and 2

N - Nematodes

A - Alternaria alternata
    (stem canker or early blight)

T - Tobacco mosaic virus

St - Stemphylium (gray leaf spot)

(See more about plant diseases on pages 74 to 81.)

How to Grow Tomatoes from Seed

Because you might like to grow many of your tomatoes from seeds, you'll want to know the best ways to get the seeds to germinate and thrive. Many of the more unusual tomato cultivars are only available as seeds, so you must learn to nurture the seeds to maturity. Even though it can be as much an art as a science, it's not too hard to germinate tomato seeds. Most gardeners will have their preferred methods, and I'm sure you'll develop your own over time, but I'll start you off with some simple steps that will guarantee a good germination rate.

In general, you'll want to germinate your seeds for six to eight weeks before the last expected frost date for your area. You can find this date on the internet by searching for "last spring frost dates." Your search will give you several choices for how to select your location, and entering your zip code may be the easiest. You'll transplant your seedlings around two weeks after this last frost date—and then nervously watch the weather for any risk of frost for another couple of weeks! If you're growing in a greenhouse, you don't need to worry about the frost. You can start your seeds according to the instructions on the packet and not have to worry about the weather unless there's an extreme cold snap and the temperature drops in your greenhouse.

Buy good-quality, sterile seed compost or seed-starting mix, and either fill individual peat pots or trays with the soil. Plant the seeds about a quarter of an inch deep, spacing them at least half an inch apart if you're growing them in trays. In pots, you can sow two seeds and discard the weaker of the two seedlings once they have two sets of true leaves (see page 30). Planting in larger pots allows you to avoid the process of transplanting your seedlings, but big pots take up more space. As you generally germinate a lot of seeds at once, having large pots takes up precious space in your germination area, whether it's a windowsill or greenhouse. Most of us find space is a premium when we're germinating a lot of seeds, so we tend to plant in smaller pots and transplant to larger pots when the seedlings are ready.

I strongly recommend you use a good-quality seed compost. Often cheap seed composts aren't fully decomposed and have solid clumps. Unfortunately, when a root or shoot hits one of these, it can't grow properly. Buy the best-quality compost you can afford. If you have the time, sift the compost through a compost sieve or fine-mesh screen to ensure it's very fine and contains no lumps to impede the growth of your seedlings. You can buy compost sieves for a few dollars or make your own easily enough with a wire mesh attached to a wooden frame. A mesh about three-eighths-inch square will produce a soil fine enough for tomato seedlings.

Pinch some soil over each seed, covering it carefully, and then water gently; do not soak the soil. Use a watering rosette with small holes on the spout of your watering can, or you might end up washing away the seed!

Make sure you label which variety is planted where so that you can tell them apart as they grow. There are some distinctions among seedlings of different varieties, but it can take an expert eye to differentiate between varieties when the plants are this small.

Move the container to a location where the temperature will stay between 70 and 80 degrees F (21 to 27 degrees C). It may help to loosely cover the container with plastic wrap, or if you're using a propagator or multicell seed tray, put a plastic lid on top to keep heat and moisture in and improve germination rates. Watch out for condensation forming on the inside of the plastic or tray lid, as this can cause the seeds to rot. Remove the lid or plastic wrap, wipe as much condensation away as you can (carefully),

and replace, ensuring there's sufficient air circulation. It's very important that the air can circulate around the seedlings; damp foliage can encourage fungal disease, which can kill your baby plants.

Your seedlings will germinate in about seven to ten days, and you'll see the cotyledon or baby leaves. At this point, the plants need exposure to a sunny window or fluorescent bulbs to give them plenty of light. Rotate the plants regularly when they start to lean toward the light to ensure they grow straight. If you're using artificial lights, place the lights directly above the plants and move them up as the plants grow to keep the leaves from being singed by the heat of the lamps. If the light is uneven or not strong enough, your plants can become leggy, meaning the stem has become too long and narrow to support good growth. If your seedlings do become too leggy, repot them into larger pots, bury as much of the stem as you can, and place the plants in more direct, even light. Tomatoes will grow new roots from the stem, which will help support the portion of the stem above the soil.

After two weeks, the baby leaves should have a good green color. If they don't, the seedlings aren't getting enough light. Your options are to find better exposure using another window; put them outside in a sunny, sheltered spot during the day; or use artificial lights, such as LED, fluorescent tubes, metal halide, or any of the other types of grow lamps on the market..

Around the thirtieth day after planting, or when your plants are three to four inches tall, the first true tomato leaves start to appear

above the baby leaves. It's best to wait until this point to transplant your seedlings to ensure they'll be vigorous enough to survive. You'll use a process called "pricking out" to move them to larger, individual pots so they have room to grow properly. This is a simple process, although you have to be very careful and gentle, as it's easy to damage your seedlings. They're very delicate at this stage, and too firm a grip on the stem can cause irreparable damage.

Hold the seedling by the true leaves and scoop up the soil from beneath it, including the entire root ball. A kitchen fork works well for this and does not damage the roots or the seedlings.

If you've planted your seeds in trays, you may find that the roots of the seedlings have grown together. In this case, gently tease the seedlings apart, being careful not to damage the plant. It isn't so much of a problem if you break a root or two, but ideally you want to cause as little disruption as possible. Be especially careful of the stem and leaves, as damage to them is often irreparable. If the plants are too close together to pull apart, you'll either have to destroy one seedling by cutting its stem with scissors or pinching it off or leave them growing together.

Transplant each seedling into a container that's around three to four inches in diameter and filled with a good-quality potting mix. Poke a hole in the soil for the seedling, making sure it's large enough for the root ball to fit, and ensure all of the roots are below the surface of the soil. The seedlings need to be planted deeply enough that the baby leaves are just slightly above the surface. Placing some of the stem into the soil will encourage root growth along that part of the stem and ensure your plants will be more sturdy and vigorous. Make sure the soil is firm around the stem so the plant will have support during growth.

Don't water the seedlings from above, but carefully water the soil around each of them and avoid soaking the seedling itself too much. Give them enough water that it starts to run out the bottom of the pot, and only water when the soil has dried. (Push your finger into the soil down to the first knuckle and see if it feels wet at the tip of your finger. If it does, don't water.) Keep newly transplanted seedlings out of direct sunlight for a couple of days, so they can recover from the move and establish their root systems.

Seedlings are growing rapidly at this time, so they'll benefit from a liquid feed once a week; use a tomato feed or any general purpose fertilizer. Some experts advise to wait until the plants start to fruit before feeding, but giving the plants a boost at the seedling stage will encourage plenty of healthy growth. Any tomato feed will have the right balance of nitrogen, potassium, and phosphorus to ensure your plants grow well and produce a good crop of tomatoes. Nitrogen will encourage stem and leaf growth, phosphorus will favor flower growth, and potassium will support the plants once the fruits are set. Give them a feed with too much nitrogen and they'll become spindly and produce a lot of leaves, but not many flowers.

If you garden in a cool climate, you may want to transplant your seedlings once more into four- to six-inch pots when they're eight to ten inches tall, especially if your greenhouse germination space is getting crowded. If you have a particularly short growing season, giving your plants room to grow indoors for a longer period of time will allow them to get well established before planting outdoors and help them get off to a running start once they're in your garden.

Once the low temperatures at night reach a minimum of about 55 degrees F (13 degrees C), it's time to start hardening off your plants, helping them adjust to outdoor conditions. This avoids the shock a plant will experience from being moved from the comfortable and relatively even temperatures inside your house directly into the range of temperatures that can occur early in the growing season. Too much of an adjustment can delay the growth of a tomato plant by several weeks, which could make the difference between getting and not getting a good crop. In a worst-case scenario, the shock of suddenly being abandoned to the outside world can kill your delicate seedlings. Just to be on the safe side, you may want to place large baskets, plastic buckets, or garden pots over the plants or use fabric row covers over them if there's a risk of a late frost. Keep a close eye on the local weather forecast and protect your plants if it looks like temperatures will dip below 50 degrees F (10 degrees C), even if frost is not predicted. Remove the covers, especially from baskets and pots, the next day once temperatures start to warm.

About three or four days before you start to harden off your plants, stop fertilizing them and reduce the amount of water you're giving them until they're planted outside. Then, over the period of a week to ten days, move your plants outside into the sun for a few hours each day. Every day gradually increase their exposure to the weather until they're in the sun all day long. At the end of ten days, leave the seedlings out overnight to acclimatize them to being outside full time.

Once the seedlings have been hardened off, it's time to plant them in the garden, in larger pots, or in grow bags (see page 48). Prepare them first by removing the bottom true leaves from any plants taller than six inches, so you can plant more stem below ground and encourage extra root formation and a more stable adult plant.

I'll discuss planting your tomatoes outside here but will cover how to grow tomatoes in containers on pages 47 to 51. Also, be sure to read about preparing your garden bed on page 56, so the condition of your soil will be to your tomatoes' liking.

Dig the hole where the tomato plant will be located, making sure that it's large enough to accommodate the root ball and any extra stem; remove any noticeable stones from the hole and break up the soil in the bottom a little. Leave twenty-four to thirty-six inches between the plants, depending on the variety, to allow for good air circulation and access for pruning and harvesting. This will look like a lot of space when the plants are small, but as they grow, they'll fill in this distance rapidly.

Tip the plant out by spreading your fingers into the famed Vulcan sign from *Star Trek* (a V for the non-geeks) and putting the stalk between your fingers. Tip the pot upside down and either tap the bottom of it or squeeze the sides of the pot so the entire root ball drops

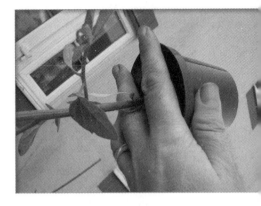

into your hand. Your fingers will support the stem and prevent damage to the plant.

If you do this while the plant is dry, it slips out fairly easily; do this outside or over a tray as some soil may break loose in the process. Some people prefer to water their plants first because the soil is then bound to the roots and the plant may suffer from less transplant shock. From personal experience, either method will work, and the process you choose will be a matter of personal preference. I usually don't water before this step because I don't want to get my hands too coated in mud, and it's

a lot easier to remove a dry root ball from a container than a damp one. If your seedlings are in peat pots or other biodegradable pots, they don't have to be removed before planting. Tear or cut off at least the bottom of these pots so the plant roots won't struggle to get through the container.

Place the seedling into the hole you dug so the lowest set of leaves are just slightly above the soil. Fill the hole with soil and firm it down, making sure the plant is straight and upright. See page 37 for information on different types of support you can use to keep your tomato vines off the ground. Inserting these supports sooner rather than later will help your plants grow upright and prevent possible damage to stems and roots. Water the plant thoroughly at the base of the plant, avoiding the leaves. It's worth my mentioning several times throughout the book that damp tomato leaves are more prone to blight and other disease, so let the rain do its job and only water at ground level. If the plant leans after watering, tamp down the soil around the plant firmly to straighten.

To maximize your yield, include a range of varieties from early fruiters, midseason fruiters, and late-season fruiters. If there's a particular variety that's a favorite, plant a few seeds every couple of weeks, instead of all of the seeds at once. This way your tomatoes will ripen at different times, and you won't be overloaded with a glut.

What to Look for When Choosing Tomato Seedlings

Not everyone has the space to grow tomatoes from seed; sometimes life happens and you don't get time to start from scratch or your seeds fail to germinate. Buying tomato seedlings from a grower is an excellent alternative. Using seedlings is also useful if you've had problems germinating seeds or some disaster has befallen your young plants. Be aware that the selection of varieties will be limited compared to the types of seeds you can find, and you may struggle to find colored or unusual varieties. You'll also need to ensure that the plants you purchase are healthy so they'll thrive when you get them home. You're looking for strong plants that are upright; avoid plants that have yellow leaves, or have damaged leaves or stems. Larger garden centers will offer more options, and smaller stores may feature heirlooms or more offbeat choices.

Avoid plants that have grown too leggy or tall or have wilted, yellowing, or otherwise damaged leaves or stems. These signs of stress may mean the plants haven't gotten enough light or have been overcrowded. You may be drawn to tall, spindly plants, thinking they'll grow more quickly once in your garden, but the stems are weak and will break easily when they're put outside or are heavy with fruit. You'll get the best results from short, stocky plants with thick stems. The ideal tomato seedling is between eight and ten inches in height, with a strong, thick stalk and robust, deep green leaves.

Local seedling growers are usually motivated to provide varieties that will grow well in their areas to ensure their customers' success. This should also be the case at large garden centers, but double-check the growing information provided on the plant identification label. The "days to maturity" listed on the label is the time the first fruits should appear, roughly estimated from the time the grower expects you'll plant the seedling; this should be well before your first frost date. The longer the period between the days to maturity and the average first frost, the longer your harvest will be. (If you're growing tomatoes in a greenhouse, this will be less relevant.)

People often make the mistake of buying their seedlings too early in the season. Commercial growers will entice you with lush seedlings as soon as they think planting outdoors is feasible, but this might be too early for your exact location. While you may be able to keep these plants alive indoors in pots, you'll struggle to provide good conditions for them unless you're putting them in a greenhouse. Hold off purchasing seedlings until no more than a week or two before you plan to put them in your garden.

Hardening off your purchased tomato seedlings is as important as hardening off homegrown seedlings. Follow the information on this on page 32.

How to Care for Your Tomatoes

Tomatoes that are well cared for will produce a delicious, abundant crop of fruit. You'll increase your chances of a successful harvest by ensuring the plants aren't damaged by pests or diseases, and this doesn't necessarily have to take a lot of time. If you've followed the instructions for planting seedlings, they should be strong, healthy, and off to a good start.

The Best Soil for Your Tomatoes

Although tomatoes will grow in almost any environment, you have to have the right sort of soil to get an abundant quantity of tasty fruit. Tomatoes like fertile loam and sandy loam soils that are fairly loose, well drained, and high in organic matter. They don't do very well in dry soil, but they also don't like to be in soggy soil, so avoid planting them in an area that holds water or where water stands after it has rained. Tomatoes really dislike heavy clay; if you have clay soil, you'll need to mix in enough compost, peat moss, sand, sawdust, or other organic material to loosen it up without making it too moist.

Dig in some good-quality compost to create a loose, fertile soil. Adding some sand will help to improve drainage; work it into the top twelve to eighteen inches of soil. Unless you have a very heavy clay soil, you shouldn't have to work the soil any deeper than this. If you do, try planting in raised beds to lift the top roots of the plant out of the heavy clay. Over time, you can work in organic material to loosen up the clay, but it can take a few years for the soil quality to improve.

The acidity level of the soil (or pH level) is important for tomato plants. They grow best if the soil is neutral (pH 6.5) or close to neutral. You can buy pH testing kits at your local garden store or online. If necessary, change the pH level your soil so it's more neutral. Add agricultural lime to the soil to increase the pH level or ammonium sulfate or elemental sulfur to lower the pH level.

Wildlife and plant life

Because deer and rabbits will enjoy helping themselves to your beautiful plants and fruit, you may need to build a fence around your vegetable garden. If deer are prominent in your area, your fence should be at least six feet high; if rabbits are a problem, opt for mesh fencing that's anchored into the ground. Dig rabbit fencing twelve to twenty-four inches into the ground to prevent the rabbits from digging under the mesh and getting to your plants.

Supporting Your Tomatoes

A n indeterminate tomato plant produces vines that would, in a natural environment, creep along the ground. This type of tomato should be grown upright to prevent mold from developing on the stems and fruit and to discourage slugs, snails, and other ground pests from damaging the fruit. Bush or determinate tomatoes only require support in certain situations (see page 39). Tumbling tomatoes don't require support as the fruits are small in proportion to the size of their vines. Vining tomatoes that are grown upright need to be carefully supported to prevent their branches from breaking under the weight of their fruit, particularly beefsteak tomatoes whose individual fruits can weigh a couple pounds each. Growers of giant tomatoes will make hammocks for each of the large fruits to support them and prevent the stems from snapping under their weight.

There are several methods for staking your tomatoes upright, and the best method for you will depend on conditions in your area (weather, the location of your garden site) and personal preference. Tomato plants that are exposed to the elements require sturdier support than those grown in a greenhouse or polytunnel. I'll address two main types of supports: upright poles and surrounding supports.

Many gardeners use bamboo canes because they're easy and inexpensive to obtain. Bamboo is such a renewable resource, it's often my first choice. Canes are usually available in lengths from four to ten feet; you can use the shorter lengths for small bush tomatoes (if their fruits are large and need support) and the longest ones for indeterminates grown indoors. Canes from six to eight feet are good for outdoor vining plants. If you use other types of wood stakes, try to find hardwood, which will hold up to moisture and not toe. Look for stakes that are an inch square or more to provide solid support. Some gardeners also use metal poles; they can last for many years although they're heavier than wood and prone to rust.

Even if you don't tie the plant to the support immediately, put the support in place as soon you plant the tomatoes in the ground or move

them to their final container. Any support system that will be anchored below the surface of the soil will be driven through the root system of the plant and may cause damage. If you don't set surround-support systems in place until your plants are several feet tall, you risk damage to stems, flowers, and fruit when you do put them in position.

Some gardeners like to use small canes or supports when the plant is small and taller, thicker canes as the plant develops. While this can work, you're constantly disturbing the plant's root system, which makes it vulnerable to attack by diseases or pests. Although it may look peculiar to see a twelve-inch tomato plant with a six-foot cane next to it, you won't have to disturb your plant as it's growing.

Cane supports should be pushed into the ground one to three inches away from the main stem, taking care not to damage the stem itself. The support needs to be close enough to the plant that it can be easily tied but not so far away that the ties bend the stem. Push the cane at least six to twelve inches into the ground, using the greater depth if you know you're likely to get high winds or a heavy crop of tomatoes.

Once the cane is in place, tie the main stem to the cane. Use a soft garden twine; avoid plastic garden twine, as this tends to fray, and you'll end up with long pieces of plastic in your soil for years to come.

Tie the support to the stem in a figure eight with the twine crossing between the stem of your plant and the support (see image below). Tie it tightly enough to support the plant, but not so tightly that it damages the stem. The stem is going to grow thicker, and you'll need to cut the string and tie it again as your plant grows. You'll also need mul-

tiple ties as your plant grows taller, usually spaced anywhere from six to twelve inches apart, depending on where the plant needs support. I tend to place ties just below a leaf joint; the leaf then rests on the tie and provides a bit of extra support.

Although determinate (bush) tomatoes require less support, I recommend a single cane in place to support the central stem when growing outside, as they're still susceptible to wind damage. Sometimes you can end up with a bumper crop, and the plants do need extra support for the offshoot branches in that case.

Use bamboo canes where required, and tie branches to the canes. With larger bush tomatoes, you can end up with several canes supporting various branches!

SUPPORTING OUTDOOR TOMATO PLANTS

When growing tomato plants outdoors, determine the length of cane you need to use. If you're in a region with warm temperatures and

a long growing season, your plants will be able to grow taller than if you're in a northern latitude with a short growing season. At a minimum, you will want six-foot canes, though in warmer areas, eight-foot canes are better because your plants can grow that tall before you'll want to pinch off the tops.

In more exposed areas, bamboo canes may not be strong enough to support your plants as they could bend and break in the wind. If this is the case, use thicker supports, such as metal or the one- to two-inch stakes used for supporting young trees. These are not going to bend in the wind and, although more expensive, will protect your plants and can be used for many years.

Alternatively, you can use tomato cages to support your plants. These can be made out of bamboo canes (see cane tepees, opposite page XX) or bought from gar-

den supply stores. The cage goes around the plant, supporting it as it grows. As the plant grows, the cage can also be used to support the fruit.

If you live in a particularly exposed area where high winds and driving rains are common, you may want to consider building a windbreak, perhaps with a bamboo screen, around your tomato plants to help stop wind damage. Use something that can be moved, because you'll want to avoid growing tomatoes in the same place every year (see page 61).

SUPPORTING INDOOR TOMATO PLANTS

Plants grown either in a greenhouse or container also need to be staked to aid air circulation, to make it easier for you to tend to your plants and monitor their health, and to support the branches and fruit so no stems break or tear. The support methods used for outdoor plants apply to both greenhouse and container-grown plants as well.

Greenhouse tomatoes usually grow higher than outdoor plants, so you'll need eight- to ten-foot supports. Plants grown in containers will typically not grow to the same size as those in the soil of a greenhouse (unless you're using very large pots), so four-foot canes will usually do for them. Insert your supports as soon as you transplant your tomatoes. With container tomatoes, insert the support into the soil until it hits the bottom of the container. Follow the general information about tying up your outdoor plants (see opposite page) for your indoor or container plants.

BUILDING A CANE TEPEE

You can also build cane tepees to support your tomatoes. They're similar to tomato cages, but since they're built into the ground, it's easier to construct them where you plan to grow your tomatoes and then plant one tomato under each structure.

You will need these materials:

- 6 eight-foot bamboo canes
- Garden twine
- Scissors

1. Push the canes eight to twelve inches into the ground in a circle so they are evenly spaced.

2. Bend the canes toward each other until they cross about four to six inches from the top. Tie them together at this point to form the skeleton of a tepee. You can also buy plastic bamboo

cane wigwam supports, discs you can use to push the canes through rather than tying them.

3. Once this framework is in place, plant the tomato plant in the middle of the circle.

4. Tie twine around the framework at six- to eight-inch intervals to form rings to support your plants.

5. You can also add a central cane to tie the main stem to if you want to provide extra support.

THE FLORIDA WEAVE

This method for supporting tomato plants is used commercially, but it is also handy for the home gardener who is growing multiple plants in a row in the ground.

I recommend using two-inch square wooden stakes that are between six and eight feet long, depending on how tall your tomato plants are going to grow. You can use the same twine you would use to tie the tomatoes to stakes, but it does sag as the growing season progresses and will need to be tightened regularly.

Start trellising your plants when they're less than two feet tall. Once your plants are much bigger than that, it becomes harder to weave the twine around the plants without causing damage, and you run the risk of root damage by inserting stakes.

Insert a stake at either end of your row of tomato plants in line with the main stems. Then place another stake between every two tomato plants, also lined up with the main stems. (See the illustration below.)

About eight inches above the ground, loop the twine around the first stake. Then weave the twine, alternating in and out of each plant.

When you reach the final stake in the row, pull the twine tight and wrap around the stake several times. Then weave back to the first stake, again alternating in and out of each plant. Once you reach the first stake, tie it off with some knots. As your plants grow, add additional twine trellises every six to eight inches to continue to support the plants.

Feeding Your Tomatoes

Tomatoes are greedy plants and use a lot of energy to produce their fruit. If you can, buy plant food specifically formulated for tomatoes, as it has the precise balance of nutrients that tomato plants need to thrive. Otherwise, a general purpose fertilizer containing phosphorus and potassium will be beneficial. Avoid using fertilizer that's high in nitrogen, particularly after the plant has flowered, because it will stimulate lots of leafy growth and less fruit. Feed your plants regularly, according to the instructions on the package. You can use foliar feeds, applying diluted fertilizer directly on the leaves, but this is best done early in the morning so the leaves have lots of time to dry off. (See page 58 for more information on fertilizers.)

Watering Your Tomatoes

Tomatoes will suffer from irregular watering and don't like being dry. If the soil around the plants becomes very dry on a regular basis, the fruit will split and spoil. Although tomatoes don't like standing water, they do appreciate regular watering to keep them moist.

The best way to water is around the base of your plants and not on the leaves. Watering the leaves can encourage diseases, such as blight and molds. It's also better to water in the morning rather than the evening because the plants will bring up moisture into the stem and fruits during the day. Watering in the evening often leaves your plants wet at night, which also increases the risk of developing disease.

It's better to give your plants a good soaking every few days than a quick drink every day. Superficial watering encourages surface rooting, which leads to a plant that will blow over far too easily. You'll want to get water down deep to the plant roots, which encourages stronger root growth and results in healthier, better-supported plants.

Invite industrious insects by planting some French marigolds near your toma-toes; as companion plants, they'll encourage the presence of pollinators and discourage pests. (See more about companion plants on page 65.)

Pruning and Pinching Out

Before flowers appear, a tomato plant concentrates its energy on producing leaves. Eventually, it will need more branches to hold more leaves so it can grow even bigger.

If you're growing indeterminate or vining tomatoes (also known as cordon tomatoes), new branches will grow from side shoots or suckers that develop in the crotch between a leaf and the stem. (Bush or

determinate tomatoes don't grow side shoots.) As the season progresses, the plants will rapidly put out more suckers and stems.

Don't be tempted to let these side shoots grow, or you'll end up with an unwieldy, untidy plant, a giant triffid that produces few quality fruits because so much of the energy of the plant is diverted to growing green-ery. Either the plant will become too big, and spindly branches will start to break under the weight of the fruit, or the plant will succumb to fungi, mold, and bacteria because air circu-lation through the branches is poor.

Pruning helps the tomato plant concentrate its energies on producing fruit once flower clusters (trusses) begin to appear. It's much easier for both you and the plant if you remove the sucker shoots when they're small, though they will sometimes get away from you as you can see in the picture on page 44. (Be warned that tomatoes grow rapidly, and this will need to be done every few days during the growing season.)

Grasp the bottom of the sucker between your thumb and forefinger (see photo at right) and pinch it, using your fingernail if necessary. It should come off very easily. Alternatively, use a sharp knife or a pair of pruning sheers to cut the sucker off. It might be better to use these tools, as you can tear the stem when removing these side shoots by hand, which can lead to the introduction of disease.

Discard the sucker; don't leave it on the ground at the base of your tomato plant because it will rot there and encourage the spread of disease and pests. Similarly, if you damage a leaf in the process, you'll need to remove it so it doesn't attract disease-producing organisms into the rest of the plant.

If your plant has side stems or suckers below the first fruit cluster or truss that appears on the plant, they need to be removed. You'll also want to remove some of the lower leaves at this time to enable light and air to get to the fruits at the bottom of the plant. Don't go crazy as the plant needs leaves to survive and grow, but removing some of them will help with air circulation and prevent diseases from taking hold.

In warmer climates, be careful not to overprune your tomatoes; without enough shade, your fruit can suffer from sun scald. Likewise, in damper climates, you need to be especially careful to regularly prune your plants because moisture will cause problems with your plants and encourage disease. Dead leaves at the bottom of a plant provide a welcome home for slugs and snails that'll happily eat your tomatoes for you.

When a tomato plant matures, the lower leaves start to turn yellow and will drop off the plant eventually. Pinch these off by hand when you notice this happening to prevent disease, improve the plant's appearance, and keep the plant focused on producing fruit. Discard spent leaves immediately, and regularly check for leaf debris at the base of your plants; remove this as well, discarding it rather than adding it to your compost as it could harbor pests and disease.

Free tomato plants from side shoots

Everyone loves something for free. Quite often you'll overlook a side shoot and it will grow quite large, four to five inches perhaps. If you do, remove it with your fingers following the instructions for removing suckers on page 45, but don't throw the shoot on the compost pile. Turn it into a free tomato

plant! If you have a long growing season, these secondary plants will produce late-season tomatoes; if you live in a cool climate, grow these new plants in a greenhouse or in a sunny window in order to get extra tomato plants and more fruit. Suckers at the bottom of the plant will typically be stronger because they're closer to the source of the plant's energy and sugars.

When you remove a long side shoot, remove the bottom few leaves, if there are any, so you'll have several inches of bare stalk. Place the stalk end in a glass of water on a sunny windowsill and leave it to grow roots; then you can transplant the rooted shoot like a seedling. If you add some very dilute tomato food (one part tomato food to ten parts water) to the water, it will help the shoot grow stronger. The picture above shows the root system on a tomato sucker that was put into a pot of water.

Harvesting side shoots is a great way to increase your yield and make use of something you would normally throw away. If you only have a couple of plants of a particular variety because the seedlings are expensive, this is a great way to get more plants for free.

You should also pinch off the tops of your tomato plants. Typically, this is above where four fruit trusses or clusters have formed—seven if you're growing plants in a greenhouse. You literally pinch off the top growing shoot, which lets the plant concentrate its growth on the fruits below.

In the photo at the bottom of page 45, note the top shoot, just above where you can see the flower. This is the part you remove to prevent the plant growing taller.

How to Grow Tomatoes in Containers

Many people don't have garden space for growing tomatoes, but anyone can grow tomatoes in containers. You can grow them in large pots on a deck, in special grow bags as part of your landscaping, or even in tumbling varieties in hanging baskets outside a sunny window. By cultivating heavy croppers in containers, you can grow a lot of tomatoes in a small space, whether they're on your window ledge or balcony or in a small corner of your yard. You don't need a lot of plants to produce plenty of tomatoes for eating fresh; two to four will typically be enough for most people.

When you grow tomatoes in containers, you can be more successful in areas with a short growing season because you don't need to wait until the soil outdoors has warmed before planting your seedlings. You can bring them inside if there's a sudden cold snap or the season is coming to a close. You can also move them around to take advantage of the sunniest spots. I used to bring my plants into the sunroom when there was a danger of frost, and that would extend the growing season by a few weeks.

Another big advantage of containers is that you won't have the same weed problem you would if you grew them in a garden space. It takes a lot less time to look after the plant and care for it, and harvesting is much easier too.

Although you can grow any variety of tomato in a container, bush

Grow bags

The use of grow bags was popularized by my fellow British gardeners several decades ago. Many of us use greenhouses to extend our growing season, and planting tomatoes (or any one crop really) in the same ground over and over encourages pests and disease, as well as exhausts the soil of nutrients. So gardeners caught on to the idea of laying plastic bags of potting soil on the ground, slitting across the top to open them up, and planting their seedlings directly in these bags of soil. Putting a few holes in the underside of the bag will help with drainage and prevent the bags from getting waterlogged. At the end of the growing season, the spent soil is put on your compost heap or used as a top dressing elsewhere in your vegetable patch.

When I grow tomatoes at home in grow bags, they do really well. They produce great fruit, don't grow too rampantly, and don't struggle against diseases or pests (apart from the hordes of snails that live in my garden).

A new generation of polypropylene fabric grow bags that have handles and look like large shopping bags are deeper (allowing for more root growth), portable, and can be recycled when they're no longer needed or have reached the end of their productive lives. Because the fabric will allow the soil to drain, you don't have to be as vigilant about overwatering. The handles will allow you to tote your plant to the best location for sunlight, warmth, and wind protection as the season progresses.

(determinate) varieties do best, as their growth is contained and the plants won't need to be staked. See pages 20 and 24 for the best varieties to grow in containers, though any determinate tomatoes will do very well if your environment is suitable for them. Some varieties are bred especially to grow in small containers.

THE BEST CONTAINER SOIL MIX

The soil mix in your containers needs to be good quality, otherwise your tomato plants will struggle to thrive. You want soil that has plenty of organic matter in order for it to drain well. Don't use soil from your garden because it's going to contain weeds and pests and will compact over time.

Be aware of the difference between potting soil and potting mix. Soil can often be a bit too heavy for a container and not drain well. A good potting mix will contain peat moss, vermiculite, perlite, sand, and compost, which allows it to be free draining but also to retain moisture. Premium mixes may also include fertilizer; standard mixes will be cheaper because they don't have fertilizer added. Many gardeners prefer standard mixes so they can have more control over what their plants feed on and when. You won't risk that the soil will be too high in nitrogen, which will cause excessive growth of greenery. There are concerns particularly among organic gardeners that potting mix with chemical fertilizer added will harm beneficial microorganisms in the soil.

If you're really looking for convenience, opt for prepared potting mix—but there's a price to go with the convenience factor. You can save money by making your own potting mix, which is especially cost effective if you're going to be filling a number of containers. You'll need to have the following ingredients.

- Potting soil—This can contain all sorts of additives and not surprisingly very little actual soil! You want a plain potting soil without anything added to it.

- Pearlite/vermiculite—This mineral additive helps the soil retain water and stops it from compacting.

- Sphagnum moss—Add this spongy substance to help the soil retain water.

- Decayed compost—Organic compost provides nutrients for the soil as well as aerates it.

Make sure all these materials have been sterilized, so there are no diseases in the soil that can affect your plants. Mix these ingredients in equal proportions, and moisten the mix slightly before filling your containers.

Garden experts debate about whether or not to add hydrogels (water-retaining gels or granules) to potting mix. These granules slowly release water over time, which helps to prevent the soil from drying out. They aren't a long-term solution because they do break down and can release potentially harmful by-products into your soil. If you're only using the soil for one growing season, you may be okay with it, but using it is a personal preference.

PLANTING AND GROWING CONTAINER TOMATOES

Growing tomatoes in containers is fairly easy. Once the plant is in the pot, you care for it just the same as a plant that's in the ground. To start, you want your tomato containers where they're easy to see and access. Tomato plants also need between six to eight hours of sun per day, so consider that when deciding where to put them.

When choosing your pot, remember that tomatoes have large root systems and need space for their roots to flourish. Ideally, you want a pot that's as large as your growing area can support, though some varieties of tomatoes (see page 24) have been bred to grow in pots and have smaller root systems.

You need to monitor the soil in the containers very carefully and make sure it doesn't dry out. You also need to be careful not to overwater the plants because that can be just as damaging as underwatering. For suitable drainage, make sure your pot has holes in the bottom to let the excess water escape. Add some gravel or stones to the bottom of the pot for some extra drainage; this creates air pockets so the roots aren't swamped with water. Just make sure the excess water isn't going to drain off somewhere inconvenient for you! Don't be tempted to use circular plastic saucers under your pots. Your tomatoes could end up sitting in water, particularly after a rainstorm, which could kill your crop. You can use plastic saucers under your pots to prevent water runoff, but these have a habit of filling with water, whether from rain or from you watering the plants. Be prepared to empty these regularly as tomato plants don't like to sit in water; it causes the roots to become too wet and rot.

How to Grow Tomatoes in a Greenhouse or Polytunnel

Growing tomatoes in a greenhouse is great fun. In any area with a short growing season, raising your tomatoes in a greenhouse will allow you to start earlier in the year and finish well after the outdoor growing season is over. Because the plants are protected from the elements and in a warmer environment, you often find they produce fruit more quickly than plants grown outside; you can go from seed to tomatoes on the plate anywhere from sixty to eighty days. If you have a heated greenhouse, you can extend the growing season further or even grow all year round (though in cold areas, heating can end up being expensive). Growing some plants in a greenhouse, as well as some outdoors, can help you get a more continuous crop throughout the fruiting season.

Greenhouse-grown tomatoes will be less susceptible to fungal diseases because they'll be warmer at night, and, if you live in areas of persistent rainfall, they'll be less damp overall. In areas affected by blight, growing in a greenhouse can protect your plants or at least delay the onset of disease.

If you don't have the space or money for a traditional glass greenhouse, you can buy smaller plastic greenhouses that take up less space and cost far less. They're not as durable, but they're still useful; just be sure to site them somewhere safe from wind and secure them to the ground. One of my plastic greenhouses was ripped to shreds by high winds even though it was in what I thought was a sheltered area, so error on the side of caution. Stake it down, tie it down, and weight it to make sure it won't be carried away.

TIPS AND TRICKS FOR GROWING GREENHOUSE TOMATOES

A variety of tomato that's resistant to cracking and disease is ideal for growing in a greenhouse (see pages 22 to 23). You can buy seedlings from a local store, though you'll find more variety by purchasing seeds. Indeterminate tomatoes will continue to produce as long as growing conditions will allow (as opposed to determinates, which produce only one harvest). Dwarf varieties of indeterminates are ideal for a greenhouse because they don't take up as much of your precious space. Unless you're in a cold area, it is best not to plant your tomato seedlings in the greenhouse until you would normally plant them in the ground. The temper-

ature in the greenhouse may be only a few degrees warmer than outdoors and therefore not be suitable for tomato plants. If you have a heated greenhouse, you'll be able to plant tomatoes in it much sooner than you could in an unheated greenhouse.

It's particularly important to control the size of your plants in a greenhouse, as they can quickly grow rampant and crowd out any other plants you're growing there, so keep a close eye on them. The first year I grew tomatoes in a greenhouse, I went away for two weeks and came back to find I literally couldn't get through the greenhouse door because the tomato plants had grown so big! (It took the better part of a day to prune them, but the crop was fantastic.)

Whether you grow directly in the ground or containers will depend on how you've set up your greenhouse. Many people prefer containers simply because you can dispose of the spent soil at the end of the growing season and are not combating weeds growing up through the soil. If you're planting directly into the soil under your greenhouse, check the pH levels and adjust them accordingly (see page 37); if you're using containers, prepare the right type of potting soil (see page 49).

Because your plants won't have access to rain, they're dependent on you for water. If they're in pots, they'll dry out very quickly, so check them daily, if possible. Many gardeners set up a drip-feed water system in their greenhouses so they don't have to carry full watering cans. On hot days, pots may need to be watered more than once a day. You can find set-ups in your local garden store or online. Alternatively, you can water your plants by hand, though remember, just as with outdoor plants, morning is best and avoid getting water on the leaves, as plants are particularly susceptible to leaf burn in a greenhouse.

You can use blinds in southern latitudes to shield plants from getting too much direct sun. Some of the darker tomato varieties prefer diffused rather than direct sunlight and can lose their color a little in direct sun. Greenhouse shading comes in different grades that block out different levels of sunlight. Choose one that's suitable for the amount of light your greenhouse receives and provide the right amount of shade for your plants.

A lack of ventilation can cause condensation and high humidity, which can encourage disease. Open the doors and windows of your greenhouse to ensure there's plenty of air circulation. If you can, add automatic window or vent openers to your greenhouse. Because they contain a substance that expands and contracts based on temperature, they don't require electricity to operate. As your greenhouse warms up, the windows will automatically open; as it cools they'll gradually shut. In hotter areas, you can benefit from installing fans in your greenhouse to encourage air circulation, though this will require running electricity to your greenhouse or installing a gas-powered generator.

The feeding schedule for greenhouse-grown tomato plants should be the same as it is for those planted in soil or containers. Remember not to overfeed your plants or to use a feed with too much nitrogen, as that encourages too much leaf growth.

Tomatoes in a greenhouse still need support when they grow, perhaps more so because they grow so vigorously. Remember—if the plant spends too much time growing greenery, it won't produce much, if any, fruit, so pinch out the tops and side shoots just as you would with garden plants.

POLLINATION

Tomatoes are quite sensitive to the length of the day and need at least six to eight hours of darkness to flower. Depending on daylight conditions in your area, the plants should begin flowering about six weeks after going into the soil. You'll either need to provide access for insects to pollinate the flowers in order to get fruit or pollinate by hand. It's a lot easier if you let the insects do it. Growing some flowers in containers inside the greenhouse—or at least bringing them into the greenhouse while the tomatoes are flowering—will encourage pollinating insects in to do their job. Marigolds are a good choice, as they're beneficial to tomatoes. Leave the greenhouse doors and windows open during day so pollinators will be able to access your plants.

Even if you're encouraging nature to do the job for you by growing flowers in your greenhouse, you might notice your tomatoes aren't producing any fruit, and you may have to step in and give nature a helping hand. Pollinating by hand can be done in two ways. You can shake the tomato plant and hope for the best. This can actually work, but it's somewhat hit or miss. The second method is more reliable but requires more effort on your part. Dab a cotton swab, toothbrush, or small paintbrush on the inside of one flower, so the yellow pollen is transferred to it. Then dab this onto the next flower and the next and so on until all the flowers have been pollinated. The best results are obtained if you pollinate the plants every day at around noon.

How to Grow Prizewinning Tomatoes

I f you have fruit- and vegetable-growing contests in your area, you want to grow prizewinning tomatoes so you can join the competition. The prizes for winning are notoriety and the bragging rights of having your tomatoes selected over everyone else's. These competitions are taken very seriously by those that enter—prizewinners often keep both their source of seeds and growing secrets very close to their chests—but participating can make your hobby more enjoyable.

If you're growing tomatoes for your own dinner table, you can afford to be a little lax with them. However, if you're aiming to win a ribbon, you really need to be on the ball and care for those plants as if they were your children. Serious contest growers are obsessive, tending to their plants almost constantly, but their efforts show in the results. Over time, with the information in this section and your own trial and error, you'll come up with your own secret recipe for growing competition-winning tomatoes.

Rules for vegetable competitions vary from area to area, so you'll need to contact local contest organizers and obtain their rules and guidelines. Ideally, visit the contest before you enter to see how your competitors are presenting their tomatoes and exactly what they've grown. If you talk to the exhibitors, you may also be able to get some handy growing tips or advice on varieties, particularly if you don't reveal you're a potential competitor. Reading about these competitions is one thing, but it's only when you attend one do you truly understand what's required. A tricky part of exhibiting vegetables is learning how to present them as the judges expect them to be shown, so make sure you look over the winning tomatoes to get some tips on presentation.

Getting the fruit in perfect condition at the right time is probably one of the hardest parts of showing vegetables, as weather, pests, and diseases are often out of your control. Take care to do what you can to ensure success, and start by timing your seed germination. If you start your seeds too early, your tomatoes will be past their prime by the time the contest comes along. Tomatoes take up to eighty days to mature, depending on the variety. From the date of the contest, count back the number of days the tomato takes to mature (usually shown on the packet or found online); then you'll know roughly when to plant your tomatoes. Add a few more days if the growing season in your area is relatively short and September is a cool month. For instance, if your contest is the first week of October, you'll need to start germinating seeds around the beginning of June, compared to the eating tomatoes you'd start in April. You would probably sow some competition tomatoes every week throughout June so that you'll have plenty of fruit to choose from for the competition. Remember that a ripe tomato has a short shelf life, so timing really is everything.

Then select the seed you're going to grow. There are a lot of varieties on the market, including those that are marketed as "show" or "exhibition" quality. Exhibition seeds tend to produce plants that perform very well and grow uniformly sized fruit. If you opt for heirloom seed, you can start your own strain by saving some seeds from the most successful tomato plants and then building up your own variety of championship-winning tomatoes over time.

Take special care to germinate your seed using the techniques described on page 27. Some growers even soak their seeds for a few hours to soften the tough husks and help promote germination. Typically, you will sow your seeds in individual pots to avoid the need to transplant and expose your seedlings to shock. Contest growers will often plant a lot of seeds and choose the strongest of the resulting seedlings to grow for the competition. The rest are given away or grown for their own consumption.

Once the seeds are planted, place your pots in a warm area in the dark so the seeds can germinate. When you see the first stirrings of life, move the pots to a bright location but not in direct sunlight. You can use plastic wrap to form a mini-greenhouse over the pots to keep the soil warm and moist, but take care that there's sufficient air circulation to avoid it getting damp and rotting. Once the true leaves appear, remove the plastic wrap and use grow lamps or a sunny windowsill to give your plants all the light they need. Keep the soil moist so there's plenty of water to fuel their growth, but not so wet that the roots rot.

While your seedlings are getting started, prepare your garden bed by mixing peat moss, well-rotted manure, and compost into the area your prize tomatoes will be grown. (Mark the location if you're also working up other parts of your garden.) Because the peat moss is a little bit acidic, it will help prevent fungus growth. Until you're ready to plant your tomatoes outdoors, regularly weed this area as you don't want weeds stealing the nutrients meant for your tomatoes!

If you're growing tomatoes for exhibition, it's vital for the plants to be hardened off, otherwise transplant shock will hold back their growth and even delay fruiting, and you might miss the competition. It's also worth taking the time to build a wind shelter where you're going to harden off and plant your tomatoes. It will protect them from any potential wind damage. Bamboo screens or anything similar will work. If you're growing in a greenhouse, which many exhibitors do, then your plants will be protected.

You'll need to pinch suckers off the tomatoes (see page 45) and make sure to give the plant a lot of support. With exhibition plants, most of the fruit is normally removed, apart from the few that are considered the best and most competition worthy. I would recommend growing two main stems and pinching off everything else. This allows the plant to concentrate its energy into those few tomatoes and produce the best-quality fruit.

Pinch off the first couple of flower clusters at the bottom of the plant so the fruit won't bend the stalks and touch the ground. Regularly check new flowers and remove any misshapen or double blossoms. Thin each flower cluster to two or three of the healthiest flowers; as the tomatoes form, leave the most robust and remove the rest. If you're hoping to exhibit a vine of tomatoes, you need to leave more tomatoes on it and remove any potentially misshapen ones.

Pinch off the top of the plant and trim the plant of all excessive growth, taking special care to remove any insects and prevent fungal growth. Remove the bottom leaves to reduce the chance of disease, but retain enough leaves to provide shade for your tomatoes and energy for your plant to thrive.

Protect your plants from pests either by using netting around the plant (though please consider how your plants will be pollinated) or inserting plant collars in the soil around the base of the plant. You can make your own or get them from a garden center. Be particularly vigilant for slugs and snails, as they can damage tomatoes. At the end of the day, every little thing helps, and the more you can protect your plant and give it the edge, the better your tomatoes will be.

Once your plants go into the ground, water is vital, and you'll need to make sure they're kept evenly moist but not wet. Too much water and the fruit will crack; too little water and the tomatoes won't form properly. It may take a while for you to get this right, but keep records of what you do and work to improve your habits each year. If you can set up an automatic irrigation system, so much the better, as it will ensure your plants get exactly the right amount of water; all you'll need to do is check that it's doing its job.

Give each plant two gallons of water every week in addition to natural rainfall; if it doesn't rain or rains very little, then give it two gallons of water three times a week. Although foliage can cause water runoff, particularly for container plants, the water may not get near the roots of the plant. So check them, even if it rains a lot, to ensure they're getting enough water. Tomatoes grown in soil with a good, deep root system will have access to more water and be okay during rainy periods.

It is better to give a plant a good soaking infrequently than a little water regularly. A good soaking means the water gets down to the deeper roots, encouraging stronger growth, while a light soaking means only the top roots get water, encouraging a weaker rooted plant. This watering schedule works very well, though you may have to vary it slightly depending on your soil type and how it holds moisture.

Check moisture levels in the soil daily before watering. You can push your finger into the soil to check how wet it is. If the soil is damp an inch down, you don't need to provide any water; dryer than that and you'll need to water. You may have to water plants in containers every day, as the soil in pots dries out more quickly than garden soil. An alternative is to use a moisture meter, which will tell you exactly how damp or dry the soil is. They aren't expensive and are especially worth buying if rainfall in your area is erratic. The cost of putting one of these next to every tomato in your garden will soon add up, but if you're growing tomatoes for a competition, it may be worth it to get a few just for those plants.

Every time you water your plants, mix in a small amount of a well-balanced (20-20-20) fertilizer, which keeps the plant regularly fed and growing well. As the plant produces flowers and fruit, change this fertilizer to one with less nitrogen and more potassium, which encourages fruit growth. Some growers use their own secret feeds based on all sorts of weird and wonderful ingredients. Often these are comfrey tea, nettle tea, or even fertilizer based on worm castings. Seaweed-based fertilizers are particularly good for tomatoes due to their high concentration of micronutrients. Over time and with some experimentation, you'll develop your own fertilizers and techniques for growing exhibition-quality tomatoes.

When the weather cools, you'll need to shelter your plants. If you've planted them in soil, you'll need to put a plastic greenhouse over the top of them, being careful not to damage your plants in any way. Fasten the greenhouse securely to the ground so it can't be blown down and damage the plants. If your plants are growing in pots, you can move them into your greenhouse.

Open up your greenhouse during warmer days; even if nights are cool, a lot of heat can be generated in a greenhouse during the day and damage your tomatoes. Water your plants with warm water too, because at this point they're used to milder temperatures. If you use cold water, it will shock the plant and stop it from growing for about a week. (This is actually a technique that can help you slow down the growth of your plants until show day if you need to.)

Enjoy meeting all the other enthusiastic gardeners who attend these competitions; perhaps you'll win a trophy or two for all your hard work. Even if you don't take home a prize, you'll enjoy eating any tomatoes that aren't suitable for the competition!

Growing Organic Tomatoes

O rganic gardening can be very rewarding for both you and the environment, and more and more home gardeners are turning to organic methods because they make so much sense. Organic produce is healthier for you and tastes better, and organic gardening methods cause minimal damage to the beneficial insects in your garden and the soil. The downside of organic produce is that it's expensive to buy in supermarkets; the price reflects the demand and the lower yield on a commercial scale. Organically grown plants are more susceptible to pests and diseases because chemical sprays are not used. Yields tend to be lower because organic seeds haven't typically been bred to be highly productive. However, grow organic tomatoes at home, and they become very affordable, if not cheaper, than growing nonorganically!

Admittedly, in today's society it's almost impossible to be strictly organic. Chemicals can enter your growing environment by wind or rain, but you can minimize your deliberate use of chemicals and be as organic as you possibly can.

For an organic garden, you need plenty of full sun; lots of sunshine will encourage vigorous growth and reduce the incidence of pests or disease. You may need to lop the top of a few trees or switch your garden around a bit, but it'll be worth it.

You also need to fortify your soil with organic matter, particularly if your soil has a high level of clay or is rocky (remove the stones for best results). You can use compost, either homemade or store-bought, though one of the best materials is well-rotted horse manure. This can be obtained for free from pretty much any horse owner—they will (literally) be up to their knees in it and be overjoyed that someone wants to take it off their hands! Dig it in well, and it will feed your plants as well as improve the quality of your soil. If the manure is fresh, it must be set aside for up to a year to break down before you can use it safely. Fresh manure is hot as it rots down, and this heat will damage or even kill your plants.

If you want to be strictly organic, you will buy organic seeds, which are usually more expensive than standard seeds. Organic seedlings are usually only available from specialty plant nurseries, but again, typically at a premium price. Many varieties are not available in organic form, so you may not be able to find the ones you want. Most gardeners will buy standard seeds, which are relatively cheap, and grow them using organic methods. This way you get the benefits of organic gardening without some of the cost, and if you can save your seeds to grow the following year, you'll end up with your own organic seeds.

The nonorganic materials that potentially are the most harmful to you and your family are fertilizers, pesticides, and fungicides. You can buy organic versions of these and even make your own at home. Personally, even though I'm not trying to be strictly organic, I avoid nonorganic pest and disease controls until I've exhausted organic methods and need something stronger. I always use organic fertilizers such as horse manure and chicken manure (this in pellet form or fresh). These are readily available and often free; remember, animal owners are keen to get rid of it because they have so much!

Your soil is full of microorganisms and bacteria that are essential for healthy plant growth. When nonorganic chemicals are used, they often kill these important organisms and damage the health of your soil. Intensively farmed areas end up with dead, lifeless soil. Although the effect on your soil may not be so extreme, it will still have a negative effect. You'll have much healthier plants and soil when using organic products.

Weed control is the one area where you may be tempted to use nonorganic methods, but regular hoeing and weeding by hand will keep down weeds. If you spend a few minutes each day hoeing in between your plants, you won't have a weed problem. Many weeds germinate early in the growing season, so if you're diligent at the start, you'll only have a few rogue or late-season weeds to combat. With plants that have long taproots, such as dandelions, you can put a pinch of salt in the middle of the plant to kill it off. You may need to repeat the application a few times to completely kill it, but this method is effective. Just be careful not to do this too much in one area, as salt in the soil can be detrimental to your plants.

Growing through a high-quality weed membrane or ground cloth can help keep the weeds down, as can putting down a good mulch. No-dig gardening is a very good method for keeping weeds down. Turning your soil encourages weeds to grow, as seeds that are under the ground are exposed to light; no-dig gardening greatly reduces this problem. But whatever you do, regular weeding is by far the best and easiest way to keep control of the weeds. At the very least, remove the flower heads from weeds before they can seed if you don't have time to weed. This will help stop them from spreading until you can deal with them properly.

You can make your own highly effective weed killer using salt, dish soap, and white vinegar. For every pint of vinegar, mix in a good squeeze of dish soap and a teaspoon of salt. If you want a more effective weed killer, add in more salt, but remember that it can damage the fertility of your soil. This mixture is not selective the way some herbicides are, so don't get it on your vegetable plants.

Crop rotation is also going to help you because it limits or stops the buildup of pests and diseases in the soil. It also maintains the nutrient levels in the soil, as different crops have different requirements and some actually replenish nutrients. Move your tomatoes around the garden, and grow other crops where the tomatoes were, particularly brassicas or legumes. Don't grow any crops from the same family as tomatoes, such as eggplants, peppers, and potatoes, in the same location the following year. If you grow in containers, change the soil each year to prevent problems.

Companion planting is another helpful organic gardening practice (for more information, see pages 65 to 70). If you encourage beneficial insects into your garden by growing flowers, they'll not only pollinate your tomatoes but also eat many of the pests that attack them! Some gardeners think that insects are bad for the garden, yet many of them are incredibly helpful. They'll thrive on aphids and other pests, so encourage them into your vegetable patch to help organically control pests.

For me, organic methods are the only way forward. They're healthier for my family as well as being better for the environment. At the moment, we're all concerned about climate change and the negative impact humans are having on the environment. The massive decline in the bee population is linked to pesticides, which indiscriminately kill beneficial as well as harmful insects, so nonorganic methods could be a serious problem. Just imagine if there were no insects to pollinate your tomatoes—it would mean no fruit. Worse than that, if bees do die out, it would decimate the fruit and vegetable industry and create a crisis of unimaginable proportions, so every little bit the home gardener can do will help. Europe has already banned some pesticides that are thought to be contributing to the decline of bees.

Growing your tomatoes organically at home requires very little extra work on your part. It's simple, beneficial, and makes for some great-tasting tomatoes, so give it a go! Although your vegetable patch may not be vast, even being organic in a small area will make a difference.

Protecting Your Tomato Plants from Pests and Diseases

4

Diseases and pests can be a serious problem for the tomato grower. Some of them are such a nuisance that once they're in your soil, it's extremely hard to get rid of them; they can remain there for years. Some pests and diseases can decimate your plants, a heartbreaking experience after you've spent all that time and effort nurturing them.

If you've followed the guidance in this book so far, you'll have protected your tomatoes from most of the common problems. But no matter what you do, you have no control over what diseases may find their way onto your plants or which pests are transported into your garden. There are some basic practices you can adopt for managing any garden plants to reduce the chance of these problems happening and becoming serious: watering at the base, applying mulch, and leaving adequate room between your plants. There are also things you can do to prevent pests and diseases that are particular to tomatoes.

Watering

Make sure to water directly on the ground above the roots. You should never water the leaves or fruits; this keeps the plants damp and can encourage leaf mold and fungus growth. Watering the leaves or fruits can also cause sunburn, which damages the plant and stunts its growth. In addition, watering the leaves tends to direct less water to the roots because it runs off away from the base of the plant; the roots need that water to draw up nutrients from the soil into the plant.

Tomatoes benefit from small amounts of water applied regularly. If you live in a dry climate, you may need to put down a slow-drip irrigation hose. You can also create an inexpensive slow-watering system using plastic bottles. Cut the bottom end off a large soda bottle and remove the cap. Poke some holes in the cap, fill the bottle with water, screw the cap back on the bottle, and bury the cap end of the bottle in the ground at the roots of your plant. The number and size of the holes will determine how quickly the plastic bottle drains. One or two small pinholes will allow the bottle to drain gradually over the day and provide water to your tomato plant, ideal for a hot climate where plants tend to dry out during the day. Slow watering allows moisture to go directly to the roots (and can help stop weed growth by starving them of water).

Avoid watering the plants in the afternoon or evening, as soil or leaves that remain damp overnight can also encourage pests and disease. The best time for plants to be watered is in the morning because that's when they naturally suck up water; this also gives them all day to dry out. Consider this morning water as breakfast for your plant.

Mulch

Apply a two-inch thick layer of mulch at the base of your plants and about twelve to eighteen inches around them. In dry spells or hot climates, mulches are essential to keep moisture in the soil and prevent plants from drying out. Mulch also helps keep down weeds and can deter certain pests that attack the roots of your plant.

A mulch could be anything from compost to cardboard and from lawn clippings to straw or rotted leaf mold. Well-rotted manure can be used, but avoid using fresh manure; it's still composting, and the heat will damage your plants. You can use a good-quality woven weed membrane underneath the mulch to help retain moisture more effectively. Combine this with a slow-drip irrigation system, and your plants will thrive even in the driest of times.

Spacing

Make sure your plants are well spaced, as this will discourage pests and help to slow any spread of disease or pests between the plants. You need to leave twenty-four to thirty-six inches between plants; indeterminate varieties will need more space than the bush varieties. The instructions on the seed packet will also tell you the ideal spacing for the variety you are growing. It's difficult to examine plants that are planted closely together without causing some damage to them as you walk between them. Also, the plants can't get the air circulation they need to stay healthy and free of a wide variety of fungal diseases, including the dreaded blight.

By taking preventative measures and keeping a close eye on your plants, you'll be able to keep them healthy throughout the growing season. It's much better to spend a few minutes each day checking your plants than to ignore them and find you have lost your entire crop.

Companion Planting for Tomatoes

Companion planting is one of the best organic practices for keeping tomato plants healthy and reducing the risk of pests and disease. Companion planting is where two different types of plants with mutually beneficial characteristics are planted close together. (Likewise, some plants need to be kept apart, as they can cause each other a lot of problems!)

Using this traditional gardening method, you can improve the health and flavor of your tomatoes and reduce pest problems and disease. Certain plants will not only help your tomatoes grow strong and look fantastic, but are useful in their own right.

BEST COMPANION PLANTS

The following plants are known to be very beneficial to tomatoes. While it may not be practical to plant all of these, pick those that will be especially helpful considering the pests and problems in your area. Many of these companion plants will be useful in the kitchen, as well as attractive in the garden.

- **Basil.** This herb repels aphids, hornworms, mosquitoes, spider mites, and whiteflies. Its flowers attract bees, which will help

basil

  with pollination of your tomatoes. Basil also improves the health and flavor of your tomatoes (maybe that's the reason Italians commonly serve tomato with basil). For best results, pair each tomato plant with three basil plants. If growing basil with tomatoes in containers, plant it in the base of the container; if growing in garden soil, plant six to twelve inches from the tomato plant.

- **Borage.** This herb improves the health and flavor of your tomatoes, and the leaves can be used in salads. Borage will also repel cabbage worms and hornworms.

- **Chives.** Chives repel aphids, attract pollinating insects, and are delicious in salads. The purple flowers are very attractive and will be covered in bees when they are out.

borage

chives

- **Garlic.** Garlic repels spider mites. You can also use garlic as an insecticide against ants, aphids, caterpillars, slugs, whiteflies, and some beetles by making a garlic spray. Crush five garlic cloves and leave to steep overnight in a quart of water. Add four or five drops of biodegradable dish soap, then strain. Dilute in two and a half cups water, and use as a spray on your plants.

garlic

- **Marigolds.** French marigolds are some of the tomato's best companions. They repel nematodes, slugs, tomato worms, and a multitude of other garden pests. At the end of the gardening season, further deter nematodes by digging the spent marigolds into your soil.

- **Mint.** Mint deters a variety of pests, including ants, aphids, flea beetles, fleas, white cabbage moths, and rodents. Its flowers are very popular with pollinating insects, and, of course, you'll have all the mint leaves you'll need for tea. The only drawback to having mint in your garden is that it will send out runners and take over your plot. Plant it in a submerged container to keep it under control.

French marigold

mint

nasturtium

parsley

- **Nasturtium.** Nasturtiums will ward off a variety of fungal diseases and deter beetles, squash bugs, and whiteflies. It can self-seed from year to year and won't compete with your tomatoes for nutrients. Nasturtium acts as a sacrificial plant in that it attracts aphids, keeping them off your vegetables. It also produces a lovely display of flowers that are enjoyed by a wide variety of pollinating insects.

- **Parsley.** Parsley attracts hoverflies, which dine on many common tomato pests. It doesn't enjoy heat, so if you live in a warm climate, plant it where it will receive some shade at midday.

MUTUALLY BENEFICIAL COMPANION PLANTS

Some plants benefit from being grown close to each other because they provide each other benefits. Asparagus, for example, produces a chemical that kills nematodes, a pest that damages the roots of tomato plants. Tomato plants, in turn, help asparagus by repelling the asparagus beetle.

GOOD-NEIGHBOR COMPANIONS

These vegetables are good neighbors in that they'll benefit your tomatoes, helping them to thrive and grow stronger while providing you with more delicious edibles.

- **Carrots.** These root vegetables break up the ground around tomato plants, allowing air, water, and nutrients into the soil. Carrots are often harvested just after the tomatoes are planted, giving you the opportunity to use the space for something else.

- **Spinach.** In most regions, spinach will be ready to harvest when your tomatoes are going into the ground, so you can either use your spinach beds for your tomatoes or employ them for another crop.

WORST COMPANION PLANTS

These are plants that you definitely don't want to plant near your tomatoes, as they'll hinder the growth of your plants.

- **Black walnut.** Black walnut generates a compound called juglone that is toxic to tomatoes and will inhibit and stunt their growth. It can also generate walnut wilt. Very few plants grow well near walnut trees; if you have one in your garden, avoid planting anything underneath it
- **Brassicas.** The whole family of brassica—broccoli, Brussels sprouts, cabbage, cauliflower, kale, turnips—will inhibit the growth of your tomato plants.
- **Corn.** Tomatoes attract corn earworms to the corn plants, and the corn will attract tomato fruitworms to your tomatoes—so keep them well away from each other!
- **Fennel.** Fennel will inhibit the growth of your tomatoes.
- **Potato.** Planting tomatoes near potatoes will make your tomatoes more susceptible to early or late blight fungus.

FRIEND AND FOE COMPANIONS

Some plants will help tomatoes for one part of their life cycle but will harm your tomatoes in later stages of growth. When dill is young, it helps your tomatoes grow and remain healthy. However, when dill starts to flower, it will stunt the growth of your tomatoes, so remove your dill once it ages.

TOMATOES AS A BENEFICIAL COMPANION

Tomatoes can benefit other plants, so if you have any of these in your garden, you could plant your tomatoes near them to help them do better.

- **Gooseberries.** The smell of tomatoes repels insects that attack gooseberries.
- **Roses.** Tomatoes protect roses from black spot.

Companion planting is a simple way to protect your plants and help them grow. It's a natural, organic method of reducing your reliance on chemicals while protecting your plants from pests and diseases—and often the companion plants are tasty and useful in your kitchen.

Companion planting is seeing a renaissance as interest in organic, environmentally friendly gardening methods increases. These techniques have been used for hundreds of years all over the world. They may not provide complete protection, but they'll certainly reduce the incidences of problems in your garden.

Clean Garden Practices for Preventing Pests and Diseases

There's nothing worse than having your tomato crop destroyed by a pest or disease, particularly if you could have prevented it. By paying attention to the watering and feeding of your plants, as well as pinching them out and pruning them, you'll stop most of the problems and keep your plants healthy.

Check your plants daily and remove any foliage, flower, or fruit that's diseased or has pests on it. Look for discoloration on the stems, leaves, or fruit. Check for any wilting or any signs of pests, such as holes in fruit or leaves. Look under leaves, as well as in the joints between the stems and the leaves, as those are places where pests will hide. Pick off any pests that you can by hand and destroy them, which is easy to do in the early stages of infestation when the pests are small. You may want to wear rubber gloves to avoid irritation when handling some pests, particularly caterpillars. Remove dead and fallen leaves from the soil around the base of the plant; this will help to keep pests down by removing their habitat. Discard this debris or burn it; don't leave it near your plant and do not compost it. A good time to examine your plants is before daily watering.

Don't leave any plant with a problem untreated, as it can get worse rapidly and quickly go beyond the point where you can save it.

Pests and diseases also spread between plants, so treating them early stops this progression.

Growing in a greenhouse or polytunnel will help to reduce the incidences of pests and diseases. However, because it's an enclosed environment, should anything get introduced to your plants, it will spread like wildfire.

Common Pests of Tomatoes

Learn to identify the presence of common tomato pests by the damage they do.

- Chewed stem—Tomato cutworm (if early in the season)
- Defoliation—Tomato or tobacco hornworm
- Holes in leaves—Flea beetles
- Yellowing or curled leaves—Aphids

tomato cutworm

tomato hornworm

flea beetle

aphids

psyllids
leaf miners
whiteflies
spider mite

- Purpling veins in the leaves—Psyllids
- Zigzag patterns or tunnels in the leaves—Leaf miners
- Holes in the stem—Stalk borer
- White sticky residue, particularly in joints on the plant—Whiteflies or aphids
- Webbing underneath the leaves—Spider mites

On the fruit, you may see some of this damage.

- Holes in the fruit or dark pinpricks on the surface—Stink bugs or tomato fruitworms
- Discolored patches on the fruit—Stink bugs
- Holes in the fruit—Slugs

There are a number of different treatments you can use to fight these pests, and the treatment you should use depends on which pest it is. The level of infestation will also determine the treatment you decide on. Here are some common chemical-free solutions:

stink bug

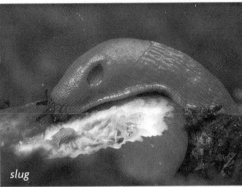
slug

Spray with water. Use a spray bottle to dislodge pests off the plants and encourage them to move on. Be careful about using too powerful a stream of water, as you can damage your plants. Spray the plants daily for a few days to get rid of as many of the insects as you can.

Handpicking. Wearing a pair of gloves, you can remove the pests by hand and drown them in a bucket of soapy water or crush them. This works well with larger pests such as hornworms. With smaller pests, such as aphids, rub your finger gently over them, which causes them to fall off or be squished. Be careful not to damage the fruit or plant, which can be difficult to avoid. Thin dishwashing gloves or latex garden gloves are often easier to use than fabric or leather gardening gloves because they give you more control over what you're doing.

Barriers. Applying a newspaper collar at the base of your plant will help to keep off cutworms.

Horticultural oils. These tend to contain a petroleum derivative or are a natural product like neem oil (from the seeds of the neem plant). Oil-based sprays block the air holes of the insect, disrupt their feeding, and inhibit growth. They can cause plant damage if not properly diluted but are very effective in getting rid of pests. Check package instructions for information on dilution rates and application instructions.

Anti-insect sprays. These are effective on pests, but ensure whatever you use is safe for an edible crop. They are usually applied by spray gun directly onto the plant and pest. Opt for an organic spray whenever possible because it won't leave harmful chemicals in your soil. A good type is insecticidal soap, which breaks down the cell membranes of the insects. These are very effective on aphids, psyllids, and spider mites. As environmentally friendly gardening has become more popular, there are many organic sprays available.

With some diseases, such as blight, and serious pest infestations, you may have no choice but to use chemicals. Be careful, as these can be toxic, usually killing beneficial insects as well as soil-based microorganisms, and they can be harmful to pets and larger wildlife. Read the instructions thoroughly and follow the application guidelines to the letter. Treat the plants according to the instructions and monitor them closely afterward. Sadly, in far too many cases, by the time you've reached this stage, the plant can be too badly damaged to recover.

Common Diseases of Tomatoes

There are a number of diseases that affect tomato plants. You can be proactive against them by purchasing disease-resistant tomatoes. Both F1 (hybrid) and heirloom varieties are available with resistant properties. If you follow watering and feeding guidelines and keep the root area free of debris, you're likely to avoid many of the diseases that usually affect tomato plants. Unfortunately, sometimes you're just unlucky, and your plants will become infected. If they do, it's important to take action immediately to prevent the disease from spreading or further harming the plant.

It is important not to confuse the term "resistant" with "immune." Tomatoes that have disease resistance can fight a disease for a while, often long enough for the fruits to mature. However, they're not immune to that disease and can still suffer from it, particularly when environmental conditions are perfect for the disease to thrive. Buying certified disease-free seeds from a reputable supplier is always a good first step in protecting your plants.

SEPTORIA LEAF SPOT

This is a very common disease caused by a fungus. It can be identified as small round spots on the tomato leaves, with a light-gray, almost white, center and dark edges. Sometimes in the center you'll see black spots. The leaves on your plant will turn yellow, wither, and eventually fall off. Long periods of warm, wet weather tend to contribute to fungal diseases like leaf spot. Raindrops spread the spores and cause the disease to infect more of your plants.

septoria leaf spot

Avoid overhead watering of your tomato plants and water at the base of the plant instead. Water in the morning, so there's plenty of time for the plant to dry out, and avoid getting water on the leaves. Prune back any leaves that are touching the ground to keep them from sitting in water.

Immediately remove any fallen leaves and burn them; do not add to your compost. If left on the plant or ground, they can encourage the spread of the disease and other pests.

To prevent this disease from taking hold and spreading, ensure there's sufficient spacing between your tomato plants. Make sure you prune them and pinch off side shoots so that air can circulate properly around the plant to dry off the leaves. There are fungicides on the market that can be used to treat affected plants, but remove all damaged foliage first.

ANTHRACNOSE

Anthracnose appears as small, round, indented areas on the fruits, and eventually rings will appear around the original spot. The fruits themselves may end up rotting, particularly if they are overripe (another reason to pick tomatoes as soon as they're ripe).

anthracnose

Like septoria leaf spot, anthracnose spores are spread by rain and splashing water and occur most often during warm, wet weather. The same procedures apply for treating this disease as for leaf spot.

EARLY BLIGHT (ALTERNARIA)

This fungus will usually attack your plant after it sets fruit. Early blight or leaf spot appears as black or brown spots with dark edges, kind of like a target. The lower leaves will be affected early on. If fruit is affected, the stem ends will show sunken black areas with concentric rings.

Early blight can be prevented by rotating your crops every year. This blight is active for a year, though the spores can remain dormant

early blight

in the soil for several years. Using blight-resistant tomato varieties will help deter infection. Planting your tomatoes in raised beds or putting containers of tomatoes on bricks will improve drainage, which can help prevent blight. Leave at least two feet between plants, and stake them upright to allow plenty of air circulation so the leaves remain dry. Do not water from above; always water the soil at the base of the plant to prevent splashing that can spread blight spores onto your plant. Mulching with a good-quality landscape fabric or black plastic will help prevent the fungus from spreading from the soil to the leaves.

There are chemical fungicides and bio-fungicides you can use to treat early blight. Apply as soon as symptoms appear, and follow the manufacturer's recommended application schedule. The longer you let blight go, the more resistant to treatment it becomes. With chemical fungicides, you'll need to check how long you have to wait after using them until you can harvest your tomatoes. A copper spray, which can be applied weekly until the leaves are dripping, is more organic. Often this will not completely clear up the problem but will stop it from taking hold and allow your plants to live longer.

Should you get blight, destroy the affected plants at the end of the growing season. Burning is the best way of getting rid of them; do not compost any diseased or infected plant material.

LATE BLIGHT

This often occurs toward the end of the growing season and is caused by cool, wet weather. It looks similar to frost damage in that it causes irregularly shaped greenish-black patches on the leaves. The fruits will rot quickly, initially developing large, irregular brown blotches.

late blight

This particular form of blight also affects potatoes, and they can cross-contaminate with tomatoes, which is why it's best not to grow these two crops near each other. If you suffer from potato blight, use varieties of tomatoes that are resistant to late blight, or plant tomatoes that mature early and are usually ready to harvest before late blight strikes. Growing early potatoes can also help, as you'll be harvesting the crop before blight strikes.

The controls for late blight are the same as for early blight. Remove all affected foliage and plants and destroy them; do not add to compost. If you have a serious problem, you may need to try a disease-resistant variety.

BLOSSOM END ROT

Blossom end rot is caused by poor growing conditions, not a pest or disease. It not only affects tomatoes, but peppers and eggplants as well. Blossom end rot shows as a circular patch, usually greenish-brown or black at the end of the fruit away from the plant. This discolored patch can vary in size, depending on the size of the tomato. The patch grows over time and becomes sunken.

blossom end rot

Blossom end rot happens when the plant doesn't get enough calcium. When a plant is deficient in calcium, cell membrane permeability is reduced. This causes the cells to swell and leak, destroying the membrane structure. New cell growth is inhibited, and a dark, sunken area appears on the end of the tomato.

A calcium deficiency in the soil is actually quite rare. The problem is caused when the plant cannot transport calcium to the fruits. The leaves, which are closer to the main stem than the fruits, receive all the calcium, leaving the fruits deficient. Plants grown in containers or grow bags are at most risk of blossom end rot because of irregular water supply. Plants grown in the soil are less likely to be affected because they have more access to water.

You may also see this problem if you've been applying too much fertilizer to your plants and the nutrients have become concentrated in the soil, restricting water uptake by the plant. Certain fertilizer ingredients, such as ammonium salts, compete with calcium to get to the plant roots, which makes the problem worse. Regularly flushing the soil with clean water containing no tomato food helps to prevent this buildup of salts. Should humidity levels be very high (which is common in a greenhouse), plants can also struggle to absorb water, which will cause a calcium deficiency. When growing in a greenhouse, good ventilation during the day is very important.

Sadly, once a fruit has blossom end rot, there's nothing you can do to save it, so remove and destroy it. However, at the first signs of this problem, there are steps you can take to prevent other fruit from being affected. Keep the soil or compost moist during the growing season, and don't allow it to dry out. During particularly hot weather or when growing under glass, you may need to water your plants several times a day to keep the compost moist. This can be difficult for many of us, so a drip-feed irrigation system can make watering duties easier. A good mulch will help retain moisture and prevent the soil from drying out. Avoid applying calcium nitrate foliar sprays, as they don't help the problem and can often make it worse; the nitrate promotes leaf growth, leaving less calcium available for the fruits.

With a good watering schedule and regular (but not excessive) feeding, your plants should avoid this disease. If you see any sign of it, take immediate steps to prevent it spreading to the rest of your fruits.

FUSARIUM AND VERTICILLIUM WILT

The most common of these two diseases is fusarium wilt, which will be found in warm climates and appear during the warmest months in cool climates. Both these diseases are caused by soil-borne fungi that prohibit water from moving between the stems and roots of plants.

This lack of water flow causes the plants to wilt on sunny days, although the plants seem to recover during the night. You'll see wilting on the top or lower leaves first, and then the leaves slowly start to lose color and die from the tips. Eventually, the entire plant is affected and will die. Your first thought is that you aren't watering the plant enough. Giving it more water causes a whole host of other problems and damages the plant. Before watering, check the soil around the plant to see if it's dry. Put your finger in the soil down to the second knuckle; if it feels damp, it doesn't need more water.

verticillium wilt

Wilt is reasonably common in heirloom varieties that haven't been bred to resist it, and some varieties of tomatoes are only resistant to one of these fungi. Look for tomato seeds that are bred to resist these diseases. These will usually be labeled V (for verticillium) and F, FF, or FFF for the fusarium variations. (See the disease resistance codes in the tables on pages 21 to 26.)

If your tomato plants are affected by these wilts, the infected plants must be removed and destroyed. Do not compost them, as the fungi spores will be spread across your soil when you use the compost. Don't use the same location for tomato plants and other nightshades (such as eggplants, peppers, or potatoes) for six years because the fungi will remain in the soil and attack those susceptible plants. Corn and beans can be planted in this area, as this fungus doesn't affect them.

MOSAIC VIRUS

This common tomato virus got its name because it produces a green and yellow mosaic on the leaves of infected plants and creates a mot-

mosaic virus

tled effect on the fruit. The leaves can also be misshapen and look more like ferns than tomatoes. Although mosaic virus doesn't usually kill a plant, it reduces its ability to produce fruits and affects their quality.

The virus will enter through any cut in leaves or stems, which is why you need to be very careful when pruning or pinching out your tomatoes. If you find evidence of the virus, reduce the risk of cross-infection by following hygienic practices. Avoid handling other plants unless you wash your hands thoroughly first, and remove and dispose of diseased plants.

You can plant varieties of tomatoes that are resistant to mosaic virus if it's common in your area. Avoid planting more tomatoes in areas of your garden where diseased plants have grown.

BACTERIAL DISEASES

There are several bacterial diseases that can affect a tomato plant, including bacterial canker, bacterial speck, and bacterial spot. These are all slightly different in nature but appear as spots on the fruits and leaves.

The same treatments used for septoria leaf can be used for these diseases (see page 74), or you can grow varieties of tomatoes that are resistant to them. Also, avoid growing tomatoes in the same area as you do peppers, as both these crops are susceptible to these diseases. Be careful about pruning or tying plants, because bacteria can enter through breaks in leaves or stems.

TOMATO PLANT DISEASE CODES

Many tomato varieties are bred for specific disease resistance, which is indicated by letters on seed packaging or seedling labels. If your packet of seeds has "VFT" on it, those seeds will grow plants with resistance to verticillium wilt, fusarium wilt, and tobacco mosaic virus.

Use the codes in the table that follows to help you determine which varieties to buy. While disease resistance can't guarantee your plants won't be affected, it does mean the plant can probably hold the disease at bay long enough to mature and produce a crop of tomatoes, particularly if they're well cared for.

CODE	DISEASE
V	Verticillium wilt
F	Fusarium wilt
FF	Fusarium wilt races 1 and 2
FFF	Fusarium wilt races 1, 2, and 3
N	Nematodes
A	Alternaria alternata (stem canker or early blight)
T	Tobacco mosaic virus
St	Stemphylium (gray leaf spot)
TSWV	Tomato spotted wilt virus

From Harvest to Table

5

The taste of a fresh tomato is something truly special, so if possible, wait to pick them until right before you're ready to use them. Once you remove a tomato from its stem, it can't get access to any more oxygen. At that point, the sugars in the tomato start to break down into ketones, alcohols, and aldehydes, which adversely affect the flavor. Supermarket tomatoes usually ripen in transit to market, at which point their sugars have almost completely disappeared. This is why the flavor of tomatoes you buy in a store rarely compares to that of your homegrown tomatoes.

Depending on the variety of tomato, fruit will be ripe anywhere from sixty to eighty-five days after planting seeds. If you plant early, mid-, and late-season varieties, you can have fresh tomatoes throughout the growing season. Hybrid tomatoes tend to ripen all at the same time, while heirloom tomatoes will ripen at different times over the season. If you're growing hybrids, have a plan for processing your bounty, be it by canning them, making soup, or preparing large batches of sauce or ketchup (see page 87).

Hybrid tomatoes are ripe when they're red on the vine; varieties that are yellow, pink, orange, or purple should transition to those colors on the vine when ripe. The entire tomato should be the same color all over, and when you squeeze it gently, it should be just on the soft side of firm. (Overripe tomatoes will be squishy when you squeeze them.) Cherry tomatoes crack if they remain on the vine for too long, so pick them just before they're ripe. Heirloom tomatoes will also be ripe a bit before they've completely turned color, so they'll also need picking a little bit early.

You can harvest tomatoes by pulling them off carefully by hand, or you can use a knife to cut the stem close to the fruit. It's best if you leave a little bit of the stem on the tomato—it helps keep the tomato fresh longer. If an entire truss is ripe, you can cut off the truss right where it attaches to the main stem. If a few tomatoes on the truss aren't fully ripe, you can cut the truss from the plant and ripen those tomatoes on your kitchen counter.

Tomatoes ripen from the inside out, so if they look ripe on the outside, they'll be ripe on the inside. Contrary to popular opinion, it's not light that tomatoes need to ripen, but heat. On warm, cloudy days, your tomatoes will continue to ripen (and if you keep them in a warm, dark cupboard, they'll still turn red!). It's only on cool days or on days when the temperature goes above 86 degrees F (30 degrees C) that they'll stop ripening. In hot climates, you may need to harvest your tomatoes before they turn completely red and ripen them indoors as they can very quickly become overripe.

Once your tomatoes start to ripen, check the plants daily, remove any ripe fruit, and use it as quickly as possible. Overripe tomatoes rot very quickly and can fall to the ground, where they'll encourage pests and disease. If you don't keep an eye on your plants, you can easily lose a lot of your crop!

Saving Your Tomato Seeds

If you're growing heirloom tomatoes, you might enjoy saving seeds to grow the following year. It's a great way to save money and continue to grow favorite varieties that are successful in your area. Seeds from these plants are much more likely to germinate and produce healthy plants the following year. After a few years of seed saving, you'll have bred a variety that's particularly well suited for your location. Seeds from F1 hybrids or supermarket tomatoes are not suitable for saving. Most supermarket tomatoes are either F1 or they've been irradiated, which means the seeds are not likely to be viable.

If you save your seeds, you'll be able to participate in seed exchanges, either with other people in your area or the many seed exchanges that have sprung up online. This is a great way to share your favorite varieties and to get unusual varieties for your own use. You can also find plants that have been bred specifically to resist disease in your area or to fruit faster.

There are several ways to remove and preserve your seeds. You can scoop the seeds out of two or three tomatoes and spread them on a piece of paper to dry. The disadvantage of this method is that the jellylike membrane that surrounds the seeds can grow mold if it isn't thoroughly dried and stored correctly. Once the seeds have completely dried, pick off any of this dried jelly, place the seeds in a paper bag, and store in a cool, dry location.

I think the best way to save seeds is through a process called fermentation. Allowing the seeds and membrane to ferment for a few days encourages the membrane to separate from the seeds as it would do in nature. Always make sure you use tomatoes that have ripened on the plant as much as possible without splitting. I'd recommend leaving a vine or two on the plant and allowing those tomatoes to ripen fully until they're close to bursting, which is when they would scatter their seeds in the wild.

Cut the tomatoes in half by holding the tomato upright and slicing down the middle of the stem end. Scoop out the seeds and put them in a small glass jar. The rest of the flesh can be discarded or put in a soup, stew, or sauce.

Cover the top of the jar with some plastic wrap, and poke a few holes in it to allow air to circulate. Place the jar in a warm place out of direct sunlight for five days. After this time, you'll see a layer of mold starting to develop. Remove the plastic wrap and use a spoon to carefully remove as much of the mold as possible.

Rinse the tomato seeds in the jar under a gentle stream of running water; most of the seeds will sink to the bottom of the jar. Either gently pour off the water or let it run off over the top of the jar. Keep doing this until the seeds are completely rinsed. You may need to use your fingers to gently loosen any tomato seeds that have stuck together. Pour off as much of the water as you can one last time.

Lay out the seeds on a coffee filter to dry. Don't use any form of kitchen towel because the seeds will stick to it and be very difficult to remove.

Keep the seeds out of direct sunlight, and leave them to dry completely. Once they're dry, remove them from the coffee filter and store them in a cool, dark place in paper envelopes or bags. Do not store them in plastic, as they'll be more prone to rotting. Check your seeds after a couple of weeks to be sure there's no mold or discoloration forming and the seeds have not been infested by insects.

Ripening Your Tomatoes Indoors

For whatever reason, you may find your tomatoes don't ripen outdoors as well as you want them to. It may be that the growing season was shorter than normal or that you were simply late planting your tomatoes, like I am most years! Another common reason is an early frost, or you planted tomatoes that take longer to mature than the length of your growing season. Most often, however, you'll experience a long stretch of bad weather, and your tomatoes won't have time to ripen.

Most tomatoes don't start ripening until daytime highs are over 55 degrees F (13 degrees C). If you live where summers are hot, your tomatoes may turn yellow or orange rather than the deep red typically associated with most varieties. If that happens, it's better to pick them while they're pink and ripen them on the vine indoors where it's cooler. Remember that ripening tomatoes need warmth but not light, so keep them inside, out of direct sunlight, in temperatures of 60 to 65 degrees F (15 to 18 degrees C).

If you feel your tomatoes are not ripening quickly enough indoors, you can speed up the process by placing them above a ripe banana or hanging a banana skin nearby. Ripe bananas give off ethylene gas, which can ripen certain foods. Commercially, ethylene gas is used to ripen tomatoes in transit from grower to store.

Tomatoes will be decimated by frost, but if the first frost is going to be a light one, you can cover your tomatoes with commercial frost covers, old sheets, burlap bags, boxes, horticultural fleece, or other material to allow you to leave the fruit on the plant a little longer—typically a few more weeks. If the frost is going to be a bad one (known as a hard or killing frost), pick all the tomatoes regardless of color. Any tomatoes that have reached three-quarters of their full size and have started to show some color will ripen indoors. The smaller green tomatoes can either be pickled or cooked. You can also pull up the entire tomato plant and hang it upside down in a warm, dark room to allow more fruit to ripen. If you do this, check the plant daily for ripe fruit before it drops and makes a mess on your floor.

Covering unripe tomatoes with newspaper will trap the ethylene gas that the tomatoes give off and help them to ripen. Check every day and remove ripe or rotten fruits. Make sure they're not touching each other to help prevent rotting.

If you're blessed to live in a warm climate, you can grow a great crop of tomatoes in the fall, though you'll struggle to find young plants to buy in the stores at this time. This is when you can make use of those suckers you removed; turn them into new plants!

Let the suckers grow to about four or five inches, then cut them from the plant with a sharp knife. To start the rooting process, remove the lowest set of leaves and place the lower end of the stem (but no leaves) in a jar of water. You can use a rooting powder, although that isn't compatible with organic gardening practices, and frankly, one thing tomatoes are very good at is producing roots.

As soon as roots have formed and are several inches long, plant the suckers in soil in pots, and water well for the next few days to encourage more root growth. These will then grow into normal tomato plants that will produce a fall crop for you. Remember that they need ample time to mature before frost arrives, so check how long it takes that particular variety to mature. Because the plant is growing from a sucker, you typically have a four- to six-week headstart on the maturity time. Keep the sucker on a windowsill or in a greenhouse to give it an advantage against cooler weather and provide time to fruit.

Preserving and Storing Tomatoes

A happy problem you might have when you grow a lot of tomatoes—especially hybrid varieties that ripen all at once—is a prodigious yield! You can very easily end up with a lot more tomatoes than you can eat fresh, but because you can't store fresh tomatoes for very long, you'll need to preserve them in order to use them later in the season. This way you can enjoy your homegrown produce all year round, which is lovely! This section will show you several ways to store your tomatoes.

CANNING TOMATOES

Canning is a great way to preserve your delicious homegrown tomatoes for use during the dark, cold months of winter. Having your own canned tomatoes brings the fresh taste of summer to your table. It's very easy to can tomatoes, and if you have older children who know how to maneuver safely around a hot stovetop, they'll enjoy helping you with the process.

The method I'll describe is called water bath canning. Special heat-resistant glass jars (usually quarts or pints) are filled with produce, closed with special canning lids rimmed with rubber seals, and set into a large pot of boiling water for long enough to kill any dangerous bacteria that might grow while the canned goods sit through the winter. Quart canning jars come with a standard opening of about 2½ inches or a wide opening ("wide mouth") of about 3 inches.

The wide mouth allows you easier access when filling or emptying the jar's contents, but the standard size will be easier to find and is totally suitable for tomatoes. The choice is yours.

You can use a pressure canner instead of a water bath canner, if you prefer, as it does cut down processing time. A pressure canner will also process your jars at a higher temperature than boiling water, which can mean less spoilage and better flavor. If you opt to use a pressure canner, follow the instructions that came with it, as the process is slightly different from what I'll describe here.

Assemble the following tools and equipment:

- **Canning jars.** A case of twelve quart jars, plus lids and lid rings, costs around ten dollars. These jars are available at many supermarkets and discount stores, especially during canning season. The lids are meant for one-time use, but the jars and rings can be used any number of times as long as they're in good condition. You can also buy extra lids separately.

- **Water bath canner.** Any very large stockpot will do, but these 21.5-quart canners are usually outfitted with a metal rack that will keep jars from knocking together and breaking while in the hot-water bath.

Typically, water bath canners cost from twenty to forty dollars.

- Large (3- to 6-quart) pot for scalding the tomatoes
- Large bowl and ice for cooling the scalded tomatoes
- Medium (1- to 2-quart) saucepan for heating liquid to fill the jars
- Small (½ - to 1-quart) saucepan for sanitizing the canning lids
- **Magnetic lid lifter.** This incredibly handy item is used to lift the lids out of the boiling water after they've been sanitized and will only cost a few dollars.
- **Jar lifter.** This is a very helpful tool to have during canning season and costs between five and ten dollars. Alternatively, you can lift the finished jars out of the hot water bath with folded towels or hot pads, but the combination of hot, steamy water and porous fabric can lead to a nasty burn if you're not careful.
- **Jar funnel.** This is another inexpensive canning tool. It's larger at the bottom than most regular kitchen funnels and fits perfectly into the opening of a standard canning jar. Most people find a jar funnel less messy to use than a regular funnel, and if you decide to can batches of homemade ketchup or tomato sauce, you'll find the wider bottom opening is essential.
- Long-handled spoons, slotted spoons, and ladles

You'll need the following to prepare approximately seven quarts of canned tomatoes:

- 20 pounds tomatoes
- ½ cup lemon juice
- 1 quart water or tomato juice

Step 1—Select the right tomatoes. Roma or paste tomatoes are particularly good because they have meatier walls and contain less water. If you plan to turn your canned tomatoes into sauce or ketchup later in the year, you'll spend less time cooking off watery juice if you start with Romas. Any other varieties can be used, though they'll typically contain more water. Also, if you use Romas or paste tomatoes, you won't have to add lemon juice to the canning jars, as these tomatoes are more acidic than other varieties.

Be sure not to use tomatoes that are overripe because at that point they're already beginning to rot. This could spoil your entire batch of canned tomatoes or, at the very least, give them a funny taste. Use firm, ripe tomatoes, leaning toward slightly underripe if you're in doubt. (Soft and squishy tomatoes can be used immediately in a cooked dish.) Avoid bruised, rotten, or mushy tomatoes; blemishes can be entry points for harmful bacteria that could grow during the months your tomatoes will be stored. If you have an overabundance of green tomatoes, you can process these without adding lemon juice because they're more acidic than ripe tomatoes.

You can weigh your tomatoes on a home bathroom scale (deducting the weight of the container the tomatoes are in), or you can hold them as you step on the scale. Step back on the scale without the tomatoes; the difference between the two weights is the weight of the tomatoes.

Step 2—Sanitize jars and lids. The easiest way to do this is in your dishwasher, particularly if it has a sanitize cycle (make sure they go through the rinse cycle to remove soap residue). If you start a batch of jars and lids while you prepare everything else, they'll be ready when you are.

Alternatively, you can boil water in a large pot (such as the canner itself) and submerge the jars in the water. Boil for a few minutes to sanitize them. Fill the canner about half full of water, cover with the lid, and heat until right below the boiling point. Heat the water or tomato juice in the medium saucepan, and start heating water in the small saucepan for the lids; they'll need several minutes in simmering water to sanitize.

Step 3—Remove the tomato skins. It's important to remove the skins from your tomatoes before canning because the skins become tough, chewy, and unappetizing when heated. Before you start going after your tomatoes with a paring knife or peeler, let me share a great trick with you. Fill the large pot halfway with water, bring to a boil, and drop in a few tomatoes at a time for thirty to sixty seconds. Remove the tomatoes with a slotted spoon, and plunge them into a bowl of ice water. The skins will slide right off, and you'll be left with naked tomatoes ready to can!

Step 4—Quarter the tomatoes and remove tough spots or blemishes. Once the skins are removed, cut the tomatoes into quarters and remove the tough sections around the stem ends. This section doesn't soften or break down well, and it will be easier to remove before the tomatoes are canned than afterward. Also remove any soft or bruised parts of the tomatoes to decrease the chance of contamination.

Step 5—Fill and top off the jars. Fill each jar with tomatoes to about half an inch of the rim. Add two tablespoons lemon juice to each quart jar (one tablespoon to each pint jar) to help the tomatoes retain their color and flavor while reducing the risk of spoilage. Then fill the jars with boiling water or hot tomato juice to within one-half inch of the rim.

Step 6—Remove air bubbles. Use the handle of a clean wooden or plastic spoon or a plastic spatula to free trapped air bubbles by sliding it around the inside edge of the jar. Carefully check to make sure there are no air bubbles so that bacteria or mold cannot grow in your jars.

Step 7—Seal the jars. Wipe the rim of each jar with a clean cloth or paper towel to ensure it's clean and dry. Moisture or debris on the jar rim will keep the lid from sealing properly. Place a sterilized lid on each jar with the rubber seal side down; secure the lids with the metal rings and screw down tightly.

Step 8—Process the jars in the canner. Set the jar rack in the canner, make sure the water in the canner is hot, and place the filled jars in the rack. If you don't have a canner rack, you can use a wire rack large enough to cover the bottom of the canner or line the bottom with a heavy towel. This will keep the jars from cracking. Add more water if necessary to cover the jars one inch, and bring the water to a gentle boil. Simmer pint jars for 40 minutes and quart jars for 45 minutes. Processing time will be shorter with a pressure canner; check the instructions that came with it for information.

Step 9—Cooling and checking the processed jars. Remove the jars, place on a wooden counter or kitchen towel, and allow to cool thoroughly without being disturbed. If you set them out overnight, they'll be cool the next morning. At this point you can remove the metal rings or at least loosen them so they don't rust and stick in place. When the jars have cooled, make sure the seal on each jar is tight. The lid should be depressed; sometimes you can even hear a pop once a seal has been achieved. If you press the center of the lid down and it pops back up again, it hasn't sealed properly. You can refrigerate that jar and use the contents in the next few days or can the contents again in a new jar, especially if you're canning tomatoes several days in a row.

When you open your jars of tomatoes, you may notice that liquid separates from the tomatoes, and you may end up with solids at the bottom and liquid at the top. Just shake the jar well before opening, and the contents will be well mixed again. This separation is perfectly normal and happens because the tomatoes were cut up before processing. When you chop tomatoes, the enzymes they contain start to break down a substance called pectin that holds cell walls together; ruptured cell walls will release liquid. This enzyme is activated by exposure to air and is inactivated by exposure to heat. When tomatoes are produced commercially, they're flash heated, which reduces this enzyme action.

FREEZING TOMATOES

Tomatoes are very easy to freeze and can be frozen whole, without any processing. Place them on baking sheets so they aren't touching and put them in your freezer. Once they're frozen solid, place them in freezer bags for storage. When you defrost or thaw them, the skins will come off very easily.

Alternatively, blanch them first, as discussed in step 3 of the canning section on page 90, and plunge them into iced water to remove the skins. Remove the tough parts around the stem ends, and put the tomatoes in freezer bags.

I find that freezing tomatoes is easier for me than canning. If I don't have much time, I can quickly freeze them whole. I have several freezers at home, so I can fill them during harvest season and switch them off once they're empty. You can also make tomato soup, sauce, or ketchup (see below) and store it in portion-sized freezer bags. I'll take tomato soup out of the freezer to use as a base for stews and other dishes.

MAKING TOMATO KETCHUP IN BULK

One of my favorite ways to preserve tomatoes is to make batches of ketchup. Ketchup (or catsup) is enjoyed by people across the world (in Europe it's often referred to as tomato sauce). The flavor of home-made ketchup is divine, and not only is it a great way to use up your tomatoes, but you also can make it according to your dietary needs: low sugar, low salt, spicy, or just distinctive. A dash of Tabasco sauce or some chilies can transform ketchup into a unique condiment.

Making ketchup at home is surprisingly easy to do, but it takes some time to prepare the tomatoes and cook them down, a great project for those occasions when you have other things to do around the house. The reward for all your hard work will be a delicious ketchup you can share with family and friends and enjoy until next year's crop of tomatoes comes in.

The following method will yield between six and seven pints. The ingredients you'll need are:

- 25 pounds tomatoes
- 1 cup chopped onions
- 1 cup sugar or sweetener of choice
- 1 garlic clove, minced
- ½ teaspoon cayenne
- Salt and black pepper
- 3 tablespoons celery seed (optional)
- Other whole or ground herbs or spices (if you have your own special recipe)
- 3 cups apple cider vinegar

Have ready the same equipment needed for canning (see page 88), plus the following:

- Colander
- Cheesecloth (if you plan to use celery seeds or any whole spices)
- Food mill or sieve
- Large (10- to 12-quart) heavy-bottomed stockpot
- 6 or 7 pint canning jars

You can purchase a food mill for about thirty dollars; it's also useful for mashing potatoes and making baby food.

Step 1—Select the right tomatoes. Weigh your tomatoes using one of the methods described in step 1 for canning on page 89. Roma tomatoes are great for ketchup, although any firm tomato with plenty of flesh will do the job. Avoid any tomato varieties that are watery, as this will affect the consistency of the final product. Avoid any rotten, bruised, diseased, or mushy tomatoes.

Steps 2—Sanitize jars and lids and remove the tomato skins. Prepare your jars and lids as for canned tomatoes on page 89, and remove the skins as described on page 90.

Step 3—Remove the seeds and membranes and drain the tomatoes. Cut the tomatoes in half, squeeze them slightly, and shake or scoop out the seeds and surrounding membrane. You don't have to remove every single seed, but get as many as you can. As you work, place the deseeded tomatoes in a colander to allow the excess water to drain off. You can save this juice to flavor soups, stews, and sauces.

Step 4—Season and simmer the tomatoes. Simmer the tomato halves, onions, sugar, garlic, cayenne, salt, and black pepper in the stockpot for 20 to 30 minutes, or until very soft. If you're using celery seeds and any whole spices, place them in the center of the cheesecloth while the tomatoes are cooking, gather the corners together, and tie the cheesecloth right above the spices with a clean piece of string. Put the vinegar and spice bag in the medium saucepan, and simmer for 30 minutes. Remove the spice bag and add more vinegar if needed to make 3 cups.

Step 5—Process and thicken the mixture. Ladle or pour the tomato mixture into the large bowl used for removing the tomato skins. Using the food mill or sieve, process the tomato mixture back into the stock-pot to get rid of any skin or seeds that remain. Add the vinegar (fla-vored, if you simmered it with the celery seeds and whole spices) to the tomato mixture, and cook over low heat at a gentle simmer until the mixture has thickened to your preference. Stir occasionally so it doesn't burn. Taste during cooking and adjust the herbs, spices, and other ingredients as desired.

Step 6—Sanitize jars and lids. Follow the steps on page 89, using the pint jars.

Step 7—Fill and seal the jars. Fill the jars to within a quarter of an inch of the rim, and wipe the rim of each jar with a clean cloth or paper towel to ensure the rim is clean and dry. Place a sterilized lid on each jar with the rubber seal side down; secure the lids with the metal rings and screw down tightly. Work quickly so the jars don't cool.

Step 8—Process the jars in the canner. Follow the instructions for processing tomatoes on page 90. Pint jars will need to be sim-mered for 35 minutes; if you prefer to use quart jars, process them for 40 minutes. Processing time will be shorter with a pressure canner; check the instructions that came with it.

Step 9—Cooling and checking the processed jars. Follow instruc-tions on page 91, being sure to immediately use up any ketchup that hasn't sealed properly.

The Best Homemade Tomato Recipes

6

I don't think any book on tomatoes would be complete without some great recipes for using them. In my first year growing tomatoes, I had more than I knew what to do with. The upside of it was I had plenty to experiment with them and tried lots of recipes. I'm sharing some of my favorites here.

Mediterranean Chopped Salad

This irresistible salad is chock-full of healthy ingredients, and it only takes thirty minutes to prepare. Use a variety of colored tomatoes for an eye-appealing variation.

1 red onion, thinly sliced

2 cups cherry tomatoes, cut in half

1 red bell pepper, chopped

1 green bell pepper, chopped

½ teaspoon sea salt

Freshly ground black pepper

1 tablespoon balsamic vinegar

1 teaspoon Dijon mustard

3 tablespoons extra-virgin olive oil

4 ounces feta cheese, cubed

½ cup fresh basil leaves, lightly packed, chopped

1 Put the onion in a small bowl and cover with cold water.

2 Put a colander over a large bowl. Put the tomatoes, red bell pepper, green bell pepper, and salt in the colander. Season with pepper to taste and toss until evenly distributed. Let sit for 20 minutes at room temperature.

3 Some juice from the tomatoes and peppers will collect in the bowl. Keep 2 tablespoons of this juice and discard the rest. Add the vinegar and mustard to the juice and whisk to combine. Slowly whisk in the oil.

4 Drain the onion and add to the bowl along with the tomatoes and peppers.

5 Add the feta cheese and basil and gently toss until well combined. Serve immediately.

Summer Tomato Salad

This simple dish takes only fifteen minutes to prepare. It's spectacular when made with freshly picked tomatoes. It's a great recipe to serve friends and family and looks as impressive as it tastes. Different-colored tomatoes will help to make this an even more exciting dish.

8 tomatoes, thickly sliced

1 cup fresh basil leaves, lightly packed, coarsely torn

¼ cup pine nuts, toasted

2½ ounces goat cheese

3 tablespoons balsamic vinegar

Sea salt

1 Arrange the tomatoes on a plate in parallel rows, with each slice slightly overlapping the previous one.

2 Sprinkle the basil leaves and pine nuts over the top.

3 Crumble the goat cheese over the pine nuts.

4 Drizzle with the vinegar and sprinkle with salt as desired. Serve immediately.

Peach and Tomato Salad

This unique combination of flavors pulls together well. The salad makes a tasty snack or side dish, or try it as a starter to impress your dinner guests. Heirloom tomatoes work best in this recipe. Feel free to use tomatoes with a variety of hues so they really stand out.

2 tablespoons extra-virgin olive oil

1 tablespoon balsamic vinegar

1 teaspoon flaked sea salt

2 ripe peaches, cut in half and sliced into half-moons

2 large tomatoes, thinly sliced

8 ounces fresh mozzarella, thinly sliced

6 fresh basil leaves

1 To make the dressing, put the oil, vinegar, and a pinch of the salt in a small bowl and whisk until well combined.

2 To make the salad, arrange the peaches, tomatoes, mozzarella, and basil in alternating layers on a serving platter.

3 Drizzle the dressing over the salad. Sprinkle the remaining salt over the top. Serve immediately.

Tomato and Watermelon Salad

MAKES 10 SERVINGS

The combination of sweet, sour, and salty flavors makes this dish a stand-out. Chill the melon in advance, but the other ingredients should be at room temperature. Prepare the salad right before you plan to serve it, as it won't hold. It's best made with heirloom tomatoes, particularly green or orange ones, although black tomatoes will offset the red watermelon very nicely.

> 4 pounds chilled seedless watermelon, cubed
>
> 3 tomatoes, seeded and cubed
>
> 1 sweet onion, thinly sliced
>
> 3 tablespoons finely chopped fresh mint
>
> 1 cup crumbled feta cheese
>
> Sea salt

1. Put the watermelon, tomatoes, onion, and mint in a large bowl and carefully toss until well combined.

2. Add the cheese and season with salt to taste. Toss gently to combine. Serve immediately.

Gazpacho

This cold soup is famous the world over, but it's surprisingly easy to make. It's very refreshing on a warm summer's day and great to serve at dinner parties. It only takes thirty minutes to make and will keep for three days in an airtight container in the refrigerator.

3 pounds very ripe tomatoes, cored and cubed

1 small red onion, cut into 1-inch pieces

1 red bell pepper, cut into 1-inch pieces

½ cucumber, peeled, seeded, and cubed

2 garlic cloves, crushed

Sea salt

4 ounces French or Italian bread, crusts removed, torn into 1-inch pieces

1 cup extra-virgin olive oil, plus more for serving

2 tablespoons sherry vinegar, plus more for serving

Freshly ground black pepper

2 tablespoons minced chives

1 Put the tomatoes, onion, bell pepper, cucumber, and garlic in a large bowl. Season to taste with salt and toss until well combined. Let rest at room temperature for 30 minutes.

2 Put a colander over a large bowl and pour the tomato mixture into the colander. The juices will drain into the bowl.

3 Arrange the vegetable mixture in a single layer on a rimmed baking sheet and put in the freezer for 30 minutes.

4 Add the bread to the juices in the bowl and stir to combine.

5 Remove the vegetables from the freezer and let rest at room temperature for 30 minutes.

6 Add the vegetables and any juices that have accumulated in the baking sheet to the bowl with the bread and stir to combine.

7   Transfer the vegetable and bread mixture to a food processor and process until smooth. You may need to do this in two or three batches depending on the size of your processor. Slowly drizzle in the oil and vinegar while processing.

8   Strain the soup over a large bowl and discard the solids. Season with salt and pepper to taste.

9   Drizzle with additional oil and vinegar before serving and garnish with the chives and additional pepper as desired.

Chilled Tomato Soup with Corn Guacamole

Tomato soup is always popular, but it's incomparable when made with home-grown tomatoes and topped with corn guacamole. This refreshing summertime recipe takes a mere thirty minutes to prepare.

SOUP

2 pounds tomatoes, stemmed and quartered

¼ cup extra-virgin olive oil

1 tablespoon red wine vinegar

½ cup fresh cilantro leaves, lightly packed

½ teaspoon sea salt

Freshly ground black pepper

CORN GUACAMOLE

1½ cups fresh corn kernels (about 2 cobs)

1 tablespoon extra-virgin olive oil

1 avocado, coarsely chopped

1½ tablespoons chopped fresh cilantro, plus more for garnish

1 tablespoon finely chopped red onion

1 tablespoon freshly squeezed lime juice

1 teaspoon finely chopped jalapeño chile

Sea salt

Freshly ground black pepper

1 To make the soup, put the tomatoes in a food processor and process until smooth.

2 With the processor running, drizzle in the oil. When the mixture has emulsified, add the vinegar.

3 Pour the soup into a bowl. Add the cilantro and salt. Season with pepper to taste and stir until well combined. Cover and refrigerate until thoroughly chilled, about 2 hours.

4 To make the corn guacamole, preheat the oven to 400 degrees F. Line a baking sheet with parchment paper or a silicone mat.

5 Spread the corn in a single layer on the lined baking sheet and drizzle with the oil. Bake for 15 minutes, until the corn is golden brown.

6 Put the avocado, cilantro, onion, lime juice, and chile in a medium bowl. Add the corn and season with salt and pepper to taste. Stir until well combined.

7 Pour the soup into four bowls. Top each serving with a generous dollop of the corn guacamole and garnish with additional cilantro.

Fresh Tomato Soup

MAKES 6 SERVINGS

Tomato soup is one of my favorite ways to use the tomatoes I grow. I make a large amount and freeze it to enjoy all year long. If you like to add cream to your tomato soup, do so when you are reheating it (not before you freeze it). This takes about thirty-five minutes to make.

4 cups chopped tomatoes

2 cups vegetable broth

1 onion, sliced

4 whole cloves

2 tablespoons butter

2 tablespoons all-purpose flour

2 teaspoons sugar

1 teaspoon sea salt

1 Put the tomatoes, broth, onion, and cloves in a large soup pot and stir to combine. Bring to a boil over medium-high heat, decrease the heat to medium, and simmer, stirring occasionally, for 20 minutes.

2 Run the soup through a food mill into another large saucepan or bowl. Discard the solids remaining in the food mill.

3 Put the butter in the empty soup pot and melt it over medium heat. Stir in the flour to make a roux and cook, stirring frequently, until medium brown.

4 Gradually whisk in a few tablespoons of the tomato mixture, ensuring there are no lumps. Add the remaining tomato mixture and stir until well combined.

5 Add the sugar and salt and cook, stirring occasionally, until heated through, 5 to 10 minutes. Serve immediately or cool and freeze.

Green Tomato Chutney

Chutney is a terrific way to use up an abundance of green tomatoes. It's particularly delightful spread on cheese sandwiches. Although the chutney takes a while to cook, it's a breeze to make.

¾ cup light brown sugar

1 pound plus 5 ounces green tomatoes, quartered

¾ cup raisins

⅔ cup white wine vinegar

1 red chile, finely chopped

1 piece (¾ inches) fresh ginger, peeled and grated

1 shallot, finely chopped

1 clove garlic, finely chopped

1 Put the brown sugar in a large saucepan and cook over medium-high heat, stirring frequently, until it melts and caramelizes.

2 Add the tomatoes, raisins, vinegar, chile, ginger, shallot, and garlic and bring to a boil.

3 Decrease the heat to medium-low and simmer, stirring occasionally, until the chutney has thickened, 1 to 2 hours. When you can draw a wooden spoon along the bottom of the pan and it leaves a channel that doesn't fill up with liquid right away, you'll know it's ready.

4 Spoon into sterilized jars. Let cool, then cover and store in the refrigerator.

Tomato Salsa

MAKES 3 CUPS

Homemade salsa and corn chips are a perfect match, but raw veggies—such as carrot, cucumber, and celery sticks—are also delightful salsa companions. This tantalizing recipe takes only three minutes to make.

4 Roma tomatoes, diced

4 green onions, white part only, thinly sliced

1 jalapeño chile, finely chopped

¼ cup chopped fresh cilantro, lightly packed

Sea salt

½ cup cold water

1. Put the tomatoes, green onions, chile, and cilantro in a small bowl.

2. Season with salt to taste and stir to combine. Let rest until the salt dissolves, about 2 minutes.

3. Add the water and stir well.

4. Serve immediately or store in an airtight container in the refrigerator for up to 5 days.

Fresh Tomato Salsa

MAKES 3 CUPS

I adore salsa and make lots of it every year with fresh tomatoes. Feel free to adjust the amount of the jalapeño to suit your taste, or try even hotter chiles—such as habanero or Scotch bonnet—if you want your salsa to have a kick like a mule! Although you can use only red tomatoes, I prefer including a variety of colors because that makes the dish really pop.

3 cups coarsely chopped tomatoes

1 cup diced onion

½ cup chopped green bell pepper

¼ cup minced fresh cilantro, lightly packed

2 tablespoons freshly squeezed lime juice

4 teaspoons finely chopped jalapeño chile

½ teaspoon ground cumin

½ teaspoon sea salt

1. Put the tomatoes, onion, bell pepper, cilantro, lime juice, chile, cumin, and salt in a medium bowl and stir until well combined.

2. Serve immediately.

Roasted Tomato Salsa

MAKES 1½ CUPS

Here's a unique twist on standard salsa. This version has a deep, rich flavor created by roasting the tomatoes, which makes a surprising difference in the taste.

1 pound Roma tomatoes, cut in half lengthwise

1 teaspoon sea salt, plus more as needed

½ white onion, peeled and quartered

1 whole jalapeño chile

2 whole cloves garlic, unpeeled

⅓ cup chopped fresh cilantro, lightly packed

2 teaspoons freshly squeezed lime juice

Sugar

1 Preheat the broiler.

2 Put the tomatoes in a single layer on a rimmed baking sheet, cut-side up. Sprinkle evenly with the salt.

3 Add the onion, chile, and garlic to the baking sheet. Broil for 10 minutes, then turn over the garlic and chile. Broil for 10 minutes longer, or until the vegetables have started to blacken.

4 Let cool until the vegetables can be comfortably handled, about 10 minutes.

5 Peel the garlic and stem and seed the chile.

6 Put the vegetables in a food processor and pulse until finely chopped. Transfer to a small bowl.

7 Add the cilantro and lime juice and stir to combine. Season to taste with additional salt and sugar.

8 Cover and chill in the refrigerator for 30 minutes prior to serving. May be stored in an airtight container in the refrigerator for up to 1 week.

Provençal Tomatoes

This unusual, fresh-tasting dish has a French feel to it. It takes about an hour to make.

½ cup plus 3 tablespoons extra-virgin olive oil

6 tomatoes, cut in half crosswise

6 ounces ciabatta bread, torn into large pieces

1¼ cups grated Gruyere cheese

¼ cup chopped fresh parsley, lightly packed

1 shallot, finely chopped

2 cloves garlic, chopped

1 teaspoon dried thyme

1 teaspoon lemon zest

½ teaspoon crushed red pepper flakes

Sea salt

Freshly ground black pepper

1 Preheat the oven to 400 degrees F.

2 Brush a 13 x 11-inch glass baking dish with 1 tablespoon of the oil.

3 Scrape out the seeds and flesh of each tomato half very carefully, taking care not to damage the tomato skin. Arrange the tomatoes cut-side up in a single layer in the baking dish, making sure each half sits flat.

4 Put the bread in a food processor and pulse to make about 2 cups of bread crumbs.

5 Add ½ cup of the cheese and the parsley, shallot, garlic, thyme, lemon zest, and red pepper flakes and pulse until well combined. Season with salt and pepper to taste.

6 With the machine still running, drizzle in ½ cup of the oil and process until the mixture starts to clump. Divide this mixture equally among the tomato halves, pressing it down slightly.

7 Sprinkle the remaining ¾ cup of cheese over the tomatoes and drizzle with the remaining 2 tablespoons of oil.

8 Bake for about 40 minutes, until the filling puffs up and browns and the tomato skins start to split. Serve hot or cold.

Roasted-Tomato Risotto

MAKES 4 SERVINGS

Here's a tasty, healthy, Italian-inspired dish that you and your friends and family will love.

4 pounds tomatoes, quartered

2 tablespoons extra-virgin olive oil, plus more for serving

4 cloves garlic, coarsely chopped

Sea salt

6 cups vegetable broth

2 tablespoons butter

1 white onion, finely chopped

1 pound arborio rice

Freshly ground black pepper

4 ounces buffalo mozzarella, torn into chunks

Arugula or microgreens, for garnish

1   Preheat the oven to 350 degrees F.

2   Put the tomatoes, oil, and garlic in a large bowl and stir until well combined.

3   Arrange the tomato mixture in a single layer on a rimmed baking sheet and season generously with salt.

4   Roast for 30 minutes, turning occasionally, until soft and caramelized.

5   While the tomatoes are baking, put the broth in a medium saucepan and bring to a simmer over medium heat.

6   Scrape the tomatoes and their juices into a strainer or food mill and push them into a bowl to make a thick puree. Discard the seeds and skins in the strainer.

7   Heat the butter in a large, heavy saucepan. Add the onion and cook, stirring frequently, until soft, about 8 minutes.

8 Add the rice to the onion and stir until well coated. Cook until the rice starts to become translucent. Add 1 cup of the broth.

9 When the broth is absorbed, add another cup of broth and cook until it is absorbed. Repeat this process until all the broth is absorbed.

10 Taste the rice to make sure it is soft but still a little chewy. If necessary, add a small amount of water and cook the rice a little longer until it is properly cooked.

11 Season with salt and pepper to taste. Stir in the tomato puree and cook, stirring occasionally, for 4 minutes.

12 Remove from the heat, stir in the mozzarella, and cover. Let rest for 5 minutes.

13 Drizzle each serving with additional oil and top with arugula. Serve immediately.

Oven-Roasted Tomato Linguine

Like most Italian-inspired dishes, this one is both tasty and good for you, and it has the added bonus of being relatively quick to make.

4 ounces vegan ham, finely diced

2½ tablespoons extra-virgin olive oil

1 pound cherry tomatoes, larger ones cut in half

½ red onion, finely chopped

¼ cup sliced kalamata olives

1 tablespoon balsamic vinegar

2 teaspoons capers, drained and chopped

1 teaspoon lemon zest

1 clove garlic, minced

½ teaspoon sugar

Sea salt

Freshly ground black pepper

1 pound linguine

2 tablespoons chopped fresh basil

1   Preheat the oven to 350 degrees F.

2   Put the vegan ham and oil in a 13 x 8-inch glass baking dish.

3   Bake for 10 minutes, or until the ham is lightly browned. Remove from the oven but don't turn the oven off.

4   Add the tomatoes, onion, olives, vinegar, capers, lemon zest, garlic, and sugar and stir well until combined. Season with salt and pepper to taste.

5   Bake for 30 minutes, until the tomatoes have softened. Stir. Return to the oven and bake for 10 minutes longer, or until the tomatoes start to brown.

6   Cook the linguine in boiling water according to the package directions. Drain and return to the saucepan.

7   Add the tomato mixture and stir until well distributed. Cook over medium heat until heated through, about 1 minute. Add the basil and stir until evenly distributed. Serve immediately.

Baked Tomato Slices

These luscious slices take only fifteen minutes to prepare. Although this recipe makes a single serving, you can easily double, triple, or quadruple it. When making more than one serving, use a variety of colorful heirloom tomatoes for an attractive presentation.

1 tablespoon extra-virgin olive oil, plus more as needed

1 large tomato, cut into ½-inch-thick slices

1 sprig fresh rosemary, leaves removed and finely chopped

1 clove garlic, minced

Sea salt

Freshly ground black pepper

1 Preheat the oven to 350 degrees F.

2 Brush a baking sheet with the oil. Arrange the tomato slices on the baking sheet in a single layer, making sure they aren't touching.

3 Sprinkle with the rosemary and garlic.

4 Drizzle additional oil over the top and sprinkle with salt and pepper as desired.

5 Bake for 5 to 10 minutes, until the tomato slices are tender.

Fried Green Tomatoes

This is a great way to use up green tomatoes, and it's incredibly tasty. You can make this recipe with red tomatoes, but if you do, make sure they're firm and not too ripe or else they'll end up a bit mushy.

> 2 eggs
> ½ cup milk
> 1 cup all-purpose flour
> ½ cup cornmeal
> ½ cup bread crumbs
> 2 teaspoons coarse sea salt
> ¼ teaspoon ground black pepper
> 4 large green tomatoes, sliced ½-inch thick

1. Put the eggs and milk in a medium bowl and whisk until frothy and well combined.

2. Put the flour on a plate.

3. Put the cornmeal, bread crumbs, salt, and pepper on another plate and stir until well combined.

4. Dredge the tomatoes one at a time in the flour, dip them in the egg mixture, and then dredge them in the bread-crumb mixture, ensuring they are well coated all over.

5. Put about one-half inch of oil in a large skillet and heat over medium heat. When the oil is hot, fry the tomatoes in batches, making sure that they don't touch. When the bottom is brown, carefully turn them over and cook the other side until brown. Add more oil to the skillet as needed between each batch. Drain the tomatoes on paper towels before serving.

RESOURCES

IN THE US

Baker Creek Heirloom Seeds

rareseeds.com

This family-owned company offers many heirloom tomato seeds, with unusual colors and types.

Seed Savers Exchange

seedsavers.org

One of the oldest and largest seed banks, this company has hundreds of heirlooms.

Territorial Seed Company

territorialseed.com

This family-owned company tests seeds to grow in cooler climates, ensuring success anywhere.

TomatoFest

tomatofest.com

This family-owned company offers certified organic heirloom tomato seeds, including many unusual colors.

IN THE UK

Garden Organic

gardenorganic.org.uk/hsl

Heritage seed library

Plants of Distinction

plantsofdistinction.co.uk

A wide range of unusual seeds

Thomas Etty

thomasetty.co.uk/seeds

Heritage seeds and bulbs

ABOUT JASON

Jason Johns has been a keen gardener for over twenty years, having taken on numerous weed-infested patches and turned them into productive vegetable gardens. One of his first gardening experiences was digging up an entire plot that was four hundred square feet and turning it into a vegetable garden—much to the delight of his neighbors, who all got free vegetables! It was through this experience that he discovered his love of gardening and started to learn more about the subject.

Jason's first encounter with greenhouse gardening resulted in a tomato-infested jungle, but he soon learned how to grow a wide variety of plants—from grapes to squashes to tomatoes and more—in his greenhouse. (To his wife's delight, the windowsills in their house are no longer filled with seed trays every spring.) He also loves to grow giant and unusual vegetables and is still planning on breaking the four-hundred-pound barrier with a giant pumpkin.

Jason is passionate about helping people learn to grow their own fresh produce and enjoy the many benefits that come with it, from the exercise involved in gardening to the nutrients found in freshly picked produce. He often says that when you've tasted a freshly picked tomato, you'll never want to buy another one from a store again!

He's also very active in the personal development community, having written self-help books on subjects such as motivation and confidence. Jason is a qualified clinical hypnotist and has recorded over eighty hypnosis programs, which are all available from his website: musicforchange.com.

For gardening tips and advice, visit Jason at owninganallotment.com.

Click on the contact link to request his free newsletter and get notifications about his new books, as well as coupons good for 20 percent off any of the training offered.

See Jason's video diary and tips at youtube.com/owninganallotment.

Join Jason on Facebook at facebook.com/owninganallotment.

Find Jason on Twitter and Instagram as @allotmentowner.

INDEX

References for graphics and recipes are in *italic* typeface.

CANNING AND PRESERVING AT HOME
A Complete Guide to Canning, Preserving and Storing Your Produce
B06Y4FJ158 • 192 pp • $2.99

COMPANION PLANTING SECRETS
Organic Gardening to Deter Pests and Increase Yield
978-1548374754 • 116 pp • $8.95

COMPOSTING MADE EASY
Turn Your Waste into Brown Gold
B00NVNZOYK • 101 pp • $2.99

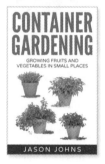

CONTAINER GARDENING
Growing Vegetables, Herbs, and Flowers in Containers
978-1517597214 • 74 pp • $7.99

COOKING WITH ZUCCHINI
Delicious Recipes, Preserves and More with Courgettes
B073TKYVNT • 128 pp • $2.99

GREENHOUSE GARDENING FOR BEGINNERS
A Complete Guide to Growing Fruit and Vegetables All Year Round
978-1539126195 • 159 pp • $9.99

GROWING FRUIT
The Complete Guide to Growing Fruit at Home
978-1502315816 • 138 pp • $7.78

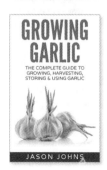

GROWING GARLIC
A Complete Guide to Growing, Harvesting & Using Garlic
978-1544042701 • 86 pp • $7.99

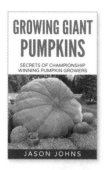

GROWING GIANT PUMPKINS
Secrets of Championship
Winning Pumpkin Growers
978-1511470384 • 86 pp • $8.99

HOW TO GROW POTATOES
The Guide to Choosing, Planting and
Growing in Containers or the Ground
978-1537555645 • 86 pp • $7.99

HYDROPONIC GARDENING
A Beginner's Guide to Growing
Plants at Home without Soil
978-1502525857 • 80 pp • $7.99

INDOOR GARDENING
The Complete Guide to Growing Herbs,
Flowers, Vegetables and Fruits
in Your House
978-1977592972 • 168 pp • $8.99

RAISED BED GARDENING
No Dig, No Bend, Highly Productive
Vegetable Gardening
978-1517138356 • 92 pp • $8.99

SQUARE FOOT GARDENING
Low Maintenance, No Dig,
Growing More in Less Space
978-1537419121 • 54 pp • $7.99

VERTICAL GARDENING
Maximum Yield, Minimum Space
Growing Plants Vertically
978-1508789956 • 46 pp • $7.99

WORM FARMING
Beginners Guide to Making Compost
at Home with Vermiculture
978-1508687429 • 62 pp • $7.99

GROUNDSWELL BOOKS
SOLUTIONS FOR A SUSTAINABLE WORLD

For more books that inspire readers to create a healthy,
sustainable planet for future generations, visit
BookPubCo.com

**The Garden Seed Saving Guide
Third Edition**
Easy Heirloom Seeds
for the Home Gardener
Jill Henderson
978-1-57067-346-7 • $9.95

How to Start a Worm Bin
Your Guide to Getting Started
with Worm Composting
Henry Owen
978-1-57067-349-8 • $9.95

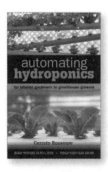

Automating Hydroponics
For Kitchen Gardeners
to Greenhouse Growers
Cerreto Rossouw
978-1-57067-366-5 • $14.95

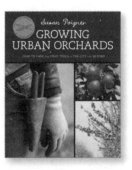

Growing Urban Orchards
How to Care for Fruit Trees
in the City and Beyond
Susan Poizner
978-1-57067-352-8 • $19.95

Purchase these titles from your favorite book source or buy them directly from:
Book Publishing Company • PO Box 99 • Summertown, TN 38483 • 1-888-260-8458
Free shipping and handling on all orders